What some are saying about this

An individual or group reading this book and using the study guide will be drinking at the well of abundant life. The treatment of forgiveness and reconciliation is pastorally wise, practically judicious, and grounded on sound use of scripture as well as the best historical scholarship. Here is a rare work of profound doctrinal substance that is simple, readable, accessible, and urgently needed.

The Rev. Dr. C. FitzSimons Allison
Retired Episcopal Bishop of South Carolina

Dr. Ellis' work communicates the truth that God reveals to us in the biblical narrative regarding forgiveness. After sharing his own journey of engagement by God and shift in understanding he uncovers the challenging process of forgiveness which will lead many readers to a similar paradigm shift. A study guide serves as a helpful accompaniment to his work. His work is thoughtful, insightful and calls the reader to a rootedness within the Christian world view and to a journey of discovery and profound Christian formation.

The Rev. Dr. Larry Kochendorfer
Parish Pastor, Ascension Lutheran Church, Edmonton, Canada

One of the key elements of forgiveness is unleashing the redemptive story of God upon ourselves and one another. So, exactly how do you do that? Larry Ellis in Forgiveness tackles this vital question for us. If you know Larry, you will not be surprised to find that his answers are thorough, Biblical and practical. I recommend it!

John White
LK10: A Community of Practice for Church Planters
http://lk10.com

Aware of the fractured relationships of those we know—and our own, could there be any more important topic than forgiveness? In an understandable, systematic, step-by-step presentation, Dr. Ellis leads us into an understanding of forgiveness that really can lead to transformed lives and relationships. I heartily recommend this book to all who want to know more fully about the kind of forgiveness that transforms.

Dr. Steven J. Hartman
Senior Minister, Third Presbyterian Church, Richmond, Virginia
http://thirdpres.org

The musician, David the Psalmist, had some important things to convey about forgiveness and reconciliation. So also does my musician friend, Larry Ellis, have much to say about forgiveness and reconciliation. It has become a passion for him. Larry's book will be a blessing. It could be God's tool for transformation in many lives. I pray it will be so.

Pastor David Morrison
Pollock Pines, California

Hal, may the Lord continue
to be blessed with you
work here.

FORGIVENESS
Unleashing a Transformational Process

Larry D. Ellis

larry.ellis@softwright.com
www.theforgivenessbook.com

FORGIVENESS
Unleashing a Transformational Process

A Study of Christian Forgiveness,
Confession, Repentance, and Reconciliation

Larry D. Ellis

Adoration Publishing Company
Denver, Colorado USA

Adoration Publishing Company
3767 South Jasmine Street
Denver CO 80237 USA
E-mail: info@adorationpublishing.com

Forgiveness: Unleashing a Transformational Process
ISBN: 978-0-9822464-0-5

Cover design and book layout: Christian Diffenderfer

Suggested Cataloging within the Library of Congress System

Ellis, Larry D., 1947-

Religion/Doctrinal Theology/Soteriology

BT795.E

1.0.1

Contents

Foreword

Human beings have developed many paradigms for achieving what they consider to be resolutions to their problems of pain, unkindness, and outright injury inflicted on them by others. These models or patterns unfortunately masquerade in people as styles of forgiveness. As a result of these pseudo-patterns for avoiding or by-passing authentic forgiveness, true reconciliation among humans often remains in a cloud of a wistful dreamland which fails to relate meaningfully to the realm of reality and so continues to be out of reach for most people. Accordingly, the world is perpetually plagued with loneliness, distrust, hostility, and violence which constantly build into explosive experiences that become justifications for various human responses of holding grudges and/or outright actions of revenge and 'get evenness'.

There is, however, an alternative way for handling our shattered feelings of betrayal, disloyalty and injury which was repeatedly disclosed in God's dealings with unfaithful Israel. Moreover, this way was most clearly revealed in Jesus, the Christ, who came into the world to provide true forgiveness for humanity's alienation and rebellion against God. In his self-giving life and sacrificial death Jesus also modeled for mortals the authentic pattern of forgiveness which can lead to genuine reconciliation. But whereas forgiveness requires only the volition of the party who has been injured, reconciliation demands the involvement of both parties in a relationship.

These topics and others have been carefully discussed in this present work by my former student, Larry Ellis, who can take his place among current writers as an authentic representative of forthright, honest evaluators who seek to challenge easy answers for difficult human concerns. He has reflected on a number of myths concerning what forgiveness is and has sought to detail why concepts of confession are often misfocused and fail to encompass the concept of agreement with God as suggested in the Bible. He has also correctly noted that repentance goes far beyond a mere change in the intellect but involves a turning around of one's entire life. In addition, he has highlighted the fact that reconciliation, which encompasses much more than getting along with those who once were not tolerated, may effectively be achieved by humans. But these issues involve the transformation of one's heart and will. You should discover in this very readable study book for the church involving forgiveness that Ellis's thinking and writing are both perceptive and stimulating. His illustrations are, moreover, captivating and clearly represent recognizable human relationships ranging from stories in the biblical period to the Apollo 11 astronauts and contemporary tragedies. The ease with which he shares his own humanness and those of others is also refreshing.

His allusions to personal and other illustrative life struggles on the pages of this book should provide an open invitation to readers to consider their own struggles with forgiveness and reconciliation. His obvious intention, therefore, is to challenge 'innovative' and pseudo-forms of forgiveness, confession, repentance, and reconciliation with the hope of encouraging others in their quest for a transforming integrity of life.

Such a desire undoubtedly harmonizes with the goal of God in the incarnation of Jesus who provided the model of genuine forgiveness which was epitomized in Jesus' declaration of forgiveness on the cross (cf. Luke 23:34) and reenacted in the death of Stephen not long thereafter (cf. Acts 7:60). Such a pattern undoubtedly had a further impact upon the fiery Paul who was the official judging agent in Stephen's execution (Acts 8:1) and who ultimately followed in the footsteps of his victim. Genuine forgiveness is not something that will go unnoticed in the world and in God's timing can have a mushrooming effect upon communities of faith and ultimately upon those around them.

As a supporter of the goals of Larry Ellis in this work, I welcome you to an intriguing journey on the pathway of forgiveness, confession, repentance and ultimately of reconciliation with God and others.

Gerald L. Borchert, Ph.D.
Retired Chair of the Biblical Division,
Southern Baptist Theological Seminary;
Thesis Director,
The Robert E. Webber Institute for Worship Studies
August 22, 2009

Acknowledgments

No author is a product only of his own making. I have been blessed with the great good fortune of having many cherished friends who have helped me see the task of writing this book through to completion. I must let it be known that a dear friend, the late Dr. Robert E. Webber, was an incalculable influence on me personally. His writings, his life, and even his death inspired me to learn to know God in a way that was more deeply personal than I had known before. My wife, Jill, has been a constant supporter of this work. In countless ways I have provided opportunities for her to practice forgiveness.

My readers have challenged me to new levels of humility. I owe a special debt to James Dodge, Harvey Powers, Frank Wells, Gerald L. Borchert, and most especially to my terrific friend and clear-minded editor, the Rev. Barbara Russo. I also wish to thank Christian Diffenderfer for his design of the book cover and for the book layout.

Last, but certainly not least, I want to thank my great friend, Fr. Christopher Ditzenberger, my pastor and one with whom I am privileged to share the life of ministry within the Kingdom of God.

All of these friends are great thinkers and practical scholars. I thank each of these inspiring people for the truly exemplary way in which they love me and strive to live consistently with what I have presented here.

Abbreviations for Biblical Books

Gen	Genesis	Jonah	Jonah
Exod	Exodus	Mic	Micah
Lev	Leviticus	Nah	Nahum
Num	Numbers	Hab	Habakkuk
Deut	Deuteronomy	Zeph	Zephaniah
Josh	Joshua	Mal	Malachi
Judg	Judges	Matt	Matthew
Ruth	Ruth	Mark	Mark
1, 2 Sam	1, 2 Samuel	Luke	Luke
1, 2 Kgs	1, 2 Kings	John	John
1, 2 Chr	1, 2 Chronicles	Acts	Acts
Ezra	Ezra	Rom	Romans
Neh	Nehemiah	1, 2 Cor	1, 2 Corinthians
Esth	Esther	Gal	Galatians
Job	Job	Eph	Ephesians
Ps	Psalm(s)	Phil	Philippians
Prov	Proverbs	Col	Colossians
Eccl	Ecclesiastes	1, 2 Thess	1, 2 Thessalonians
Song	Song of Solomon	1, 2 Tim	1, 2 Timothy
Isa	Isaiah	Titus	Titus
Jer	Jeremiah	Phlm	Philemon
Lam	Lamentations	Heb	Hebrews
Ezek	Ezekiel	Jas	James
Dan	Daniel	1, 2 Pet	1, 2 Peter
Hos	Hosea	1, 2, 3 John	1, 2, 3 John
Joel	Joel	Jude	Jude
Amos	Amos	Rev	Revelation
Obad	Obadiah		

Introduction

This book is for those who find it difficult to forgive others, after repeated, but failed, attempts. It is for those whose intuition tells them that there is still a possibility of repairing painful, broken relationships, if only one knew how to do it. It is my hope that this book serves as an encouragement to pursue the answer as to how these desires can become reality. I offer the insights presented herein as tools toward that end. Learning to forgive in this way, however, is a challenging process. We can either follow that path of discovery and Christian formation through forgiveness or we can turn away and continue as we have been living.

Although my perspectives on forgiveness may be unfamiliar, they are not of my own invention. The processes described here are fully and unashamedly rooted within the Christian worldview. I see Scripture as the record that God has delivered and preserved of his story with his creation. It describes the relationships that he initiates, has, and sustains with us and all that he has created. We must read this story understanding that it is *his* story, not ours. We must strive to see how we fit into God's story, not how God is to fit into our story. As we enter this journey into forgiveness together, I encourage you to examine whether you are doing the former or the latter. This subtle, but critical, perspective will influence how we look to the Scriptures as guidance for our actions. It will influence how we see others in relationship to us.

What I present here is found in the earliest records of biblical history. Today, many people in our Western society have lost these transformational truths, because our culture is much more human-centered (anthropocentric) than God-centered (theocentric). Therein, I believe, lies the fundamental problem. I invite you to examine carefully what I present here against the documents of history and the reality of your personal experience as you come to your own conclusions.

Should you embrace this discovery process, I suspect you will experience a paradigm shift, because it stands significantly against popular cultural understandings of forgiveness. No doubt some people will take issue with what I present here. This thinking about forgiveness likely will evoke objections not unlike those raised in response to Jesus' teaching and actions. He and his followers were clearly perceived as threats to the ruling civil authorities and the religious leadership, because his message did not follow the accepted protocols of his day. Neither can we submit to our popular cultural practices regarding forgiveness.

When we do not agree with a particular perspective, our disagreement does not invalidate the reality of its objective truth. The earth was never flat. The Nazi Holocaust is absolutely a historic fact, even though some people try to reframe it as purely fictional. Truth is never validated by the passion with which one believes it. Neither is truth invalidated because we do not believe it or agree with it. Should you reject some of my assessments, I hope that you will identify your specific objections, subject your assessments to a scholarly study and careful personal assessment, as I have attempted to do, and then be prepared to explain to anyone who asks why your alternative position is more reliable. We all must assume responsibility for our choices and actions, not simply reject a position on important matters that confront us because it makes us uncomfortable. We should make these choices freely; however, they must be informed choices. Toward that end, I offer my findings for your consideration as you strive to break patterns in forgiveness where you might be at an impasse.

Within these pages, I present some of my personal pilgrimage in learning to forgive others. On the way, my voice intersects with other voices. These voices are taken from ancient history, and includes those of influential ancient church leaders, as well as the writers of Scripture. I have included many revolutionary teachings about forgiveness by Jesus and his early followers. To these, I have added contemporary perspectives from wounded persons, whose experience with these truths has produced a freedom from control by others. I trust that my work will put forth some fresh thinking for those who struggle with forgiveness.

In this examination of forgiveness in ancient and contemporary eras, I have attempted to be both historically accurate and culturally perceptive, but by no means exhaustive. These observations will establish the foundation upon which I will compare the prevailing understandings of forgiveness in these eras. Today, much popular theology has promoted a fundamentally different understanding of interconnected words such as sin, forgiveness, confession, repentance, and reconciliation. I seek to identify and challenge some of the arenas of contemporary divergence from the ancient, Christocentric theology and practices.

The historical research presented here draws upon both biblical and extra-biblical documents from approximately the first four hundred years following the crucifixion and resurrection of Jesus Christ. The ancient Christian church grew and operated within diverse cultures throughout the Mediterranean world. The Roman Empire was vast. Regional economic, political, and historic events influenced how Christian communities differed. Yet, during this formative period, amid the ongoing transition and turmoil, the ancient church established a consistent and uncompromised theology and practice of the pivotal doctrines of forgiveness, confession, repentance, and reconciliation. I will identify representative observations and appraisals of the understanding and practices from this era, which were intended to be unalterable through time.

Relying on biblical and extra-biblical records, I will suggest how to re-appropriate certain of these ancient transformational spiritual insights regarding forgiveness. From the biblical documents, I will look at the teaching of Jesus in Matthew and the other gospels, as well as several Pauline letters. These first-hand accounts address the reality of problems within the ancient church. I will examine several texts from the Psalms, the meaning and context of which were quite familiar to the first-century Jewish Christians but unfamiliar to us today. Many of the biblical writers exhorted these new Christians and their descendants to respond to God's graceful initiatives of forgiveness and reconciliation. Hopefully, we can learn from their writings.

In the extra-biblical records, prominent leaders of the ancient churches also addressed many of the problems relating to forgiveness and reconciliation. We will read the recorded words of some of the ancient Christian martyrs, whose counter-cultural knowledge of forgiveness cost them their lives. They will bring to us not only exhortation, but also encouragement of how to live. We will look next at the prevailing understandings of forgiveness and reconciliation in today's postmodern[1] culture.

Our contemporary, secular worldview has distorted the truth of revelation widely known in the ancient world. These truths were extensively experienced by those who knew Jesus. I believe that by reclaiming the ancient transformational truth about forgiveness we

---

1. Modernity was the epoch generally arising from the Enlightenment and the Industrial Revolution. Its emphasis was logic, deemed to disclose truth. Postmodernity is the epoch of time following modernity. It is generally thought to have emerged in the late 20th century, particularly in Western culture. It is a complex, but widely held philosophy that promotes relativism in truth. In this view, absolute truth is rejected and truth is believed to exist only from the perspective of an observer. By default, truth often is arbitrated by whoever is in power. In essence, those persons who hold the reins in the government, corporate structures, and religious institutions determine what is right and wrong. When power changes hands, right and wrong also change under the new leadership. Words have no objective meaning, but instead must be reinterpreted in differing cultures, which can lead to very different and incompatible understandings.

can fulfill our hope for our desired liberation, connection, and, ultimately, intimacy with God and with one another. My desire is that all who read this book will experience God moving upon them in a transformational, new way and that they will then share their own story with those around them. Such sharing exhibits the fundamental reality of the Christian gospel.

Chapter 1

The Destructive Consequence of Innovative Forgiveness[1]

The Invitation

As we start this journey together, I hope that the story of the shift in my understanding of forgiveness will help you begin to rewrite your story. My early years of Christian formation were in good Southern Baptist churches, some small and some quite large. I faithfully participated in all the activities offered in each, especially those activities that involved worship and music. After college, I saw myself as a bit more musically sophisticated and lived a number of years in the Presbyterian world, then moved to a North American Baptist church. Finally, I graduated to the 'ultimate' of sophistication in liturgical worship and classical music, the Episcopal Church. Along the way, I had served on the staffs of many of these churches in the pastoral areas of worship and music. I had a diverse portfolio of worship leadership experience and had read many books about worship. I felt I knew quite a bit about worship. But my worship education was, to that point, essentially self-directed. I decided that to have a more effective worship ministry, I needed a formal education. My undergraduate electrical engineering degree had been earned more than thirty years previously. I made a bold decision to attend

---

1. Innovative forgiveness is a term for new and divergent understandings about forgiveness that are not consistent with the historical and biblical teachings on the subject, but which are widespread within much of our Western culture today including many Christian churches.

graduate school studying worship, theology, and Christian history. After examining the academic programs at several seminaries and universities, I selected The Robert E. Webber Institute for Worship Studies[2] and for the next several years, I commuted between Colorado to Florida to complete my classes.

I will never forget the first day at my new school. My anxiety was high. But in those first few hours on campus, during a brief worship experience at the opening presidential address, God forever changed my life.

I had come to school carrying a great deal of heaviness in my heart. I had a strong sense of betrayal by several people, who I felt were close friends. Of course, no one would have known this. I was very good at masking these feelings. I knew no one there except the president of the school, Dr. Webber. I also knew a great deal about Handel, Bach, organ literature, choral directing, thousands of Bible verses (as well as precisely what they meant for you and me!) and a great deal about group dynamics. I was especially good at exhibiting humility, which others might see and admire. When I arrived at the campus, I entered the stately, majestic, beautiful worship space of the Grace Episcopal Church in Orange Park, FL, where the presidential address would be presented to the faculty and student body. I chose to take a seat on the very front row. I wanted to experience fully everything that went on, so where better to sit than at the very front? I looked over the large space, the high altar, the beautiful stained glass, the ornate, elevated pulpit into which the preacher would ascend, and I admired the geometry and spatial design of all the liturgical areas. The beautiful carpenter (wooden) gothic architecture, the towering cathedral ceiling, the rich wood grain, the deep red and bold blue colors of the stained glass windows depicting biblical imagery, the baptismal fount midway back in the worship space all ushered me into God's presence. This environment felt a bit

---

2. The Robert E. Webber Institute for Worship Studies is located in Orange Park, Florida. See www.iwsfla.org.

mystical, and the moment filled me with a little anxiety as well as great anticipation about what might happen there.

I heard the clamor of friendly voices, although none of them were directed toward me, as I sat alone. I was okay, because the president knew me personally and I was sitting about ten feet from where he would be speaking. In a few minutes the school Provost sat down at the piano and began to play a familiar hymn, "Holy, Holy, Holy." A lover of formal, liturgical worship, I was in familiar territory. People began to quiet down and they started singing. I dutifully opened the pew hymnal and I began to sing the first verse, committed to be a fully engaged participant. The room filled with several hundred strong musical voices. I could hear all four musical parts. The music was simply incredible as we all sang robustly in the reverberant, acoustically live space. Yet, I was unprepared for what was about to happen. Something totally unfamiliar swept over me. I felt like a dam broke within me, and I began to weep profusely. I could not stop. *This is not what Episcopalians do,* I thought. We did things decently and in order, perhaps even better than the Presbyterians when it comes to worship. Yet, God was in that place and his Holy Spirit was moving upon me in some mysterious way, unlike I had ever known before. Somehow, I was now clearly worshiping, but I was no longer relying primarily upon my mind and thought processes. We finished the first stanza of the hymn and then the second verse brought me into another new experience. I literally dropped to my knees on the kneeling rail. I could no longer read the words in the hymnal because of my flowing tears. I could not control my pitch. I could hear the hymn being sung, but I could not join in. I was encountering God in a way that was totally alien to me. He had transcended my mind and was affecting my physical body, trying to get my attention about something at a much different level than that on which I normally functioned. God was unveiling all of my well-masked feelings of woundedness. I had no clue as to why this was happening or what would follow. Although I did not know it at the time, God was beginning the process of showing me a new way to live.

Having ceased my attempts to keep singing, I tried to pray. My traditional evangelical way of praying did not work. All I could say was, "Lord, I am here. Do whatever needs to be done. I want to move ahead." While the singing continued, I prayed that over and over. At that moment I made a covenant with God that I would leave no marrow on the bone, no stone unturned. I would give everything to learn all that I could from my professors, my reading, my research, my writing, and from my fellow students at my new school. I began to have a new passion to know God, unlike I had ever known before. For a long time, I had carried inside me a sense of responsibility for repairing a number of greatly stressed relationships. I wanted these relationships to be healed, but I was out of ideas about how to move ahead. I did not know *how* to forgive those who had hurt me. I had not yet experienced God taking away the masked grief and pain from my fractured heart. I was not really able to experience God's forgiveness of me. Ironically, I was working hard to please God, but was clinging to a great deal of judgment against others, who I felt were not working as hard as I was to please God. I simply saw myself as a cut above most, a legend in my own mind, as the saying goes. I had come to graduate school to learn how to do more for God. But God had brought me there to get to know him much better. In that moment of initial epiphany, I began to experience the ability to forgive others, because I knew I had been forgiven by the grace of God. I no longer had to seek it through my faithful, dutiful, proper behavior.

The contrast between these two perspectives is stark, and as time passes I see them more and more in conflict with each other. That experience of worship was the beginning chapter of a new life that continues to grow and strengthen inside me. The process of learning to accept, rather than trying to earn, forgiveness and then forgiving others continues to this day, but it is easier now than it was at the onset of my discovery process.

I invite you to take a fresh look at several important spiritual perspectives that will help unlock the ancient wisdom of God about forgiveness. My journey into forgiveness was rooted in a personal need. It remains a rewarding journey for me. I trust it will be for you as well. For some of us, it will require that we position ourselves against, rather than with, popular Western culture. This conflict between the prevailing secular culture and one's Christian faith is something that the ancient Christians knew well. But today, we Christians often have an additional layer of culture to recognize and oppose than do our friends who are not Christians.

Perhaps surprisingly, this second layer of problematic culture might be found in our own 'good' church. Churches sometimes apply simplistic formulas that miss the heart of God's teaching on forgiveness. Unfortunately, some Christians have been programmed to perpetuate a life of condemning, judgmental self-righteousness when they look at others who are not like they are. Those outside the Christian ethos are pressed only by secular influences. Those within the church must not only oppose the secular endorsement of conditional forgiveness and retribution, but also identify and oppose an embedded revisionist theology that aligns God with their own point of view. Revisionist theology can be found among 'Bible-believing', theologically conservative Christians and justice-driven, liberal Christians as well as with those who camp outside the Christian community. Additionally, many churches redefine words, changing their original meanings. Especially problematic are the words 'forgiveness', 'confession', 'repentance', and 'reconciliation'. These words must be properly understood if we are to bring restoration to broken relationships.

As you continue to read, you will be able to assess whether or not you must overcome a doctrinal problem in your understanding of forgiveness. Do not be surprised should some of your good friends find your new approach to forgiveness naïve, simplistic, or blatantly wrong. I trust that you will maintain courage and never retreat from this discovery process. This journey of transformation will always be exciting.

We Are Programmed Wrong

Very early in life, I learned that when I hurt someone, I was to say, "I am sorry." Even though I was not always truly sorry, I usually said it—eventually—especially when I was stridently exhorted to do so. I grew up knowing that I was always supposed to forgive others who either hurt me or made me angry. Unfortunately, I also learned a corollary rule: Getting angry is not pleasing to God. My outward expression of anger was somehow sinful. I believed that stuffing my feelings and being polite on the outside was more pleasing to God than blowing up. People would think more highly of me for repressing my anger, than for openly displaying it. Somehow, I would be a more 'spiritual' person because of my outward repression of internalized anger.

As I grew up, my parents and grandparents, school teachers, and the church taught me the importance of forgiveness. Surprisingly, I don't recall ever having someone talk to me about *how* to forgive someone. It seemed that saying the words properly was supposed to adjust my feelings and eventually dissipate my sadness, pain, or anger. God's word said it. I believed it. Now, it was my job just to do what it said. The good Christian life was primarily about how to behave—obedience to God. There were no Dr. Lauras, Dr. Phils, or Dr. Dobsons in our midst validating our perceptions and providing helpful advice for our consideration about how we were supposed to walk through this process of forgiveness. There was no pop-biblio-psychology, proof-texted with Bible verses, about how to raise a happy family, have a successful marriage, or orchestrate close personal relationships. Yet, somehow we all knew that forgiveness should be a regular part of our lives, especially if we were 'good' Christians.

A troublesome question with which I now wrestle is, "Why was I so nonchalant about forgiveness?" Forgiveness was my explicit theology but not my implicit practice. Forgiveness certainly was not my passion. Upon reflection, I see that it was unimportant to me for several reasons. It was not particularly difficult to dispense forgiveness to others, if they sincerely asked for it. The more humbly the offenders approached me, the easier it was to voice my gracious forgiveness toward them. Also, I felt that forgiveness from others was not particularly a big need for me, because I thought pretty highly of myself. I was an honest businessman. I was a leader and teacher in my church. I paid my taxes, loved my family, and gave money to my church. I figured that although no one is perfect, very little damage had been caused by my occasional misdeeds; after all, I had not ever really done such egregious acts as I saw in the newspapers and television newscasts. I was a pretty good person. Perhaps many people feel the same way about themselves. I have come to see this as a protective layer. By creating my own brand of self-righteousness, I protected myself from engaging others and God in a deeper way. Unfortunately, this protective process blocked me from making real connections with anyone.

For those of us who feel we should try to forgive others, the process of forgiveness can be quite difficult when someone has deeply hurt us. It is even more difficult for me to forgive someone who has hurt my children or someone else I love. Sadly, those depraved perpetrators, who are unaware, desensitized, or worse yet, downright intentionally cruel, often seem to experience no adverse consequences for their evil deeds. For that reason, it sometimes becomes my mission to make certain that justice prevails. After all, don't I believe that good people will be rewarded for their sacrificial, generous, and loving deeds, especially for helping others see the error of their ways?

As we seek to validate our distorted views, we need not look far to find outspoken reinforcement from friends, who will support all of our astute judgments about and condemnation of those miserable persons who hurt us. Such friends can unknowingly encourage our self-pity and victim mindset. Don't we all believe that those who do evil things will be punished in proportion to the sins that they have committed? That idea certainly seems fair. I might even secretly hope that those well-earned, dire consequences for these villains will come about sooner, rather than later, so that these miserable offenders can be paid back for their terrible deeds, hopefully, with interest. Perhaps then, they will be motivated to amend their ways. No less important is that we righteous ones should quickly gain the benefits of our good deeds, which we rightly deserve.

Sometimes, I could surface a meager ration of forgiveness for others, if they were willing to take full responsibility for their deeds and if they came to me and contritely asked for my forgiveness. Even then, however, I needed to feel that they were sincere or I would privately withhold forgiveness while exhibiting the outward appearance of forgiveness. This is because most of us understand forgiveness of others to be tied intrinsically to the perpetrator's remorse. Absent that, we view the other person as the obstacle to reconciliation. If the offender never takes responsibility for his hurtful actions and never asks for our forgiveness, our relationship is forever at an impasse. This understanding misses the point of forgiveness. When we make another's brokenness a precondition for our giving of forgiveness, it distracts us from focusing on our own heart and the work God wants to do there through the process of forgiveness.

Another implicit condition that we often place on our extension of forgiveness is whether or not there is the potential for ongoing relationship with the offenders. If they are no longer alive, they cannot take responsibility for their actions and in any case, the relationship cannot be restored, so we believe that forgiveness is unnecessary or impossible. If they are still alive, but they no longer matter to us, we are not likely to attempt to rebuild mutual trust in the relationship, no matter how humble their attitude is toward us. In the face of such apathy, these troubled relationships will suffer some secondary damage for which we ultimately do not feel responsible. We see ourselves as the victims. We unconsciously live in a fictional world where we always know best and see justice most clearly. We proudly assume that those fortunate enough to be in our presence should acknowledge that which is already so obvious to us. We have a grandiose vision of ourselves along with an inflated significance of self. We act out a delusional Aslan[3] persona unconsciously laced with a Walter Mitty complex.[4]

I am deeply troubled that some who proudly identify themselves as followers of Jesus can cling to and nurture unforgiveness of others for many years, feeling fully justified, because there had been no confession from the other party. In my case, this understanding was the result, at least in part, of the teaching I had received. I was taught that if we believe in Jesus, he forgives our sins. If those who hurt me believe in Jesus, their sins are also forgiven, but that process did not have anything to do with our strained friendship being reconciled. I don't recall any sermons or Sunday School classes where I learned very much about forgiveness of one another. I am certain that there was some such teaching, but somehow, I did not connect with that aspect of forgiveness in any significant way. The perspective of which I was keenly aware is that I needed God to forgive me not only for what I had personally done or not done, but because I was a fundamentally bad person and needed God's forgiveness in order to be acceptable to him. While I did learn to apologize, this was very different than actually wanting and asking someone to forgive me for what I knew that I had done wrong. The announcement of my apology allowed the hearer to remain passive with no invitation to redemptive change in our conflict. In contrast, my asking for forgiveness calls for an active response from the one who has been hurt.

---

3. Aslan was a lion in C. S. Lewis's *The Chronicles of Narnia*. He portrays the role of Jesus in the story.

4. See *The Secret Life of Walter Mitty* by James Thurber. Mitty was the mild-mannered, fictional character, who enjoyed vivid fantasies about being a killer, a fighter pilot, and an emergency room surgeon. He actually lived an inconsequential life but indulged in fantastic daydreams of personal triumphs.

Redemptive forgiveness is not a common theme in our entertainment media. Hollywood often invents and is particularly effective in perpetuating revisionist understandings of forgiveness. Extending forgiveness when one has been hurt is often portrayed as a weakness of one's character. Pastors and priests on television or in the movies seldom have keen insight or a personal character that is above reproach. Instead, they are often stooges, spineless, self-serving, greedy, or power-hungry. Worst of all, morally conscious characters in film and television entertainment are frequently portrayed as out of touch with the world around them. In our secular, sophisticated, fast-paced society the truly 'heroic' person must appear to be strong, powerful, and not controlled by anyone. In movies, the hero usually kills the most people or sleeps with the most people. He or she lives on the edge and often is the one who is smart enough to get away with deceptions and successfully carry out evil deeds. At times, a strong man or woman will rightly intervene against injustices dealt to others. Those who try to help the hurt and oppressed might well display righteous indignation against the offenders. But more often, retribution is the mantra promoted. Screenwriters portrayed such a view in the television show *Dexter*, where the police employed a mass murderer, and in the movie *The Star Chamber*, where judges secretly convened to pronounce judgment and execute penalties on 'criminals' who got off on a technicality. Payback or retaliation is the agenda; it is carried out as justice.

Even if we are so gracious as to withhold retaliation, which we feel would be fully appropriate, we still feel superior knowing that this person is morally depraved. All the while, we implicitly extol our great virtue of mercy and hope that he or she can someday come to see moral reality the way that it should be seen—*our way*. Until that time arrives, we keep our distance and hold fast to our passionate, righteous convictions, showing no sign of weakness or deviation from our high road. Perhaps our steadfastness will be the moral molding that God will use to straighten out the offender.

Certainly, not everyone is as bold and forthright as the persons described above. Nonetheless, I submit that even if you see yourself as a rather meek and mild personality, you might well operate with essentially the same judgments toward others. When mild-mannered people are hurt by others, they still place many of the same conditions on any forgiveness they might extend. We mild-mannered persons are simply much more covert in our processing and assessment. We might look more tolerant and forgiving to an observer, but these same judgmental conditions might still be present internally.

We can speak spiritual-sounding words, affirming our responsibility to 'forgive and forget' the sins of others. But in doing so, we might merely be strengthening our self-focused mindset and justifying our righteous isolation from those who hurt us. Should we unsuccessfully confront these perpetrators, some of us then seek validation in Bible verses that seem to command us to initiate this isolation. One such verse comes to mind; "If any one will not welcome you or listen to your words, shake the dust off your feet when you leave that home or town" (Matt 10:14). Because this verse is present in all three synoptic Gospels, we allow it to reinforce the propriety of our wise discernment and pronouncement of judgment against those who disagree with us. Even the Bible commands us to be separate from them! Isolation can masquerade in our spiritual unconsciousness as forgiveness, when it is more accurately the opposite—a sentence that we pass upon the other person for the judgments that we maintain against them because of our unforgiveness toward them. Do not confuse your forgiveness of someone who has hurt you with the choice of isolating yourself from them. Sometimes withdrawal is even applied to our relationship with God, as exhibited by a shut-down of communication, springing from some sense of false righteousness on our part and criticism of God's choices or his inaction. Furthermore, some of us are our own worst and most frequent accusers. We see and perhaps amplify our own shortcomings and live daily in self-judgment that continually beats us up. Receiving God's forgiveness and forgiving ourselves is a challenge, especially if our negative behavior does not seem to change. Unable to forgive our own faults, we isolate ourselves from God and others.

In all these cases effective forgiveness is never an easy process with the tools that we are normally given by our culture and many of our Christian communities.

Mirror, Mirror on the Wall

In the famous German fairy tale "Snow White," we read of the wicked step-mother who looks into her mirror and utters the words, "Mirror, mirror on the wall, who is the fairest of them all?" For many years the response was always, "You, my queen, are the fairest of them all." Because of her vanity, she believed the words. When her daughter, Snow White, grew up, the mirror told a different story, affirming Snow White's superior beauty. When the queen heard an assessment that she did not like, she was furious. She wanted it her way. It was her castle. It was her kingdom. She was the center of her reality. So it can be with us, if we do not wish to know ourselves or if we desire to dictate the rules of our relationships.

The following are stories of people who tried to rule their kingdoms. None depict any one person's life. The characters are composites, fashioned from many people who have shared with me over the years their stories of pain and woundedness. I imagine that these sketches will bring to mind some of the people that you know. This might include some persons whom you might need to forgive. But I also ask you to consider whether or not you find yourself in any of these sketches. Hopefully, these stories will help us get to the real meaning of forgiveness in challenging situations of spiritual abuse, unjust punishment, and other undeserved pain. Rejoice if you do not find yourself in these stories, but do not move quickly to identify and condemn those who come to mind as you read about those presented here. If you find yourself here, take heart, because there is a way for you to change.

I knew a popular Christian leader, Rick, who was admired by many people. Although Rick did not disclose much about any of the personal struggles in his Christian life, he was smart, handsome, and had impeccable theological credentials. His sermons were well researched and captivating. You could have an incredibly fulfilling relationship with this man as long as you agreed with him and you followed precisely what he believed to be the right path for you. He knew best on all the important things, whether it was about how to interpret a Scripture or the personal decisions that you faced in your life. He felt that he really had the trump card on other people's decision-making. He took the meaning of authority to a sinister level. In his own private way, he was very manipulative and worked tirelessly to destroy anyone around him who did not agree with his point of view. If you questioned his ideas, methods, or conclusions, you then became an obstacle that needed to be demolished. When Rick experienced conflict with someone, he attacked. He did not forgive. But, he also knew how to make you feel very good about yourself, as long as you stayed in line.

On one occasion, Rick exhorted one of his minions to resist personal pride and embrace humility under his tutelage. Rick boldly stated that he had never struggled with pride. His follower eventually came to understand the profound truth of those revelatory words meant to compliment his own stellar spiritual maturity: Rick had, indeed, never struggled with his pride. He felt fine in his contradictory life. As time passed, Rick left in his wake a seemingly endless stream of people scattered around the country, who were emotionally and spiritually undermined or destroyed by this ostensibly 'good' man. Once individuals were awakened from this man's mystique, they could only hope that they might never again be lulled to sleep amidst this type of destructive behavior.

It is very difficult to navigate through the emotional or spiritual damage caused by someone whom we respect and admire as a spiritual leader. How can one forgive Rick for the ongoing destruction that follows such a revered leader, especially should he or she continue the destructive behavior, place after place? For these vicious personal and wounding attacks, our forgiveness might seem impossible. If you are one of those whose faith in God has been undermined by such a spiritual leader, how can you then safely process appropriate faith questions with those who are in Christian leadership positions?

Another spiritual leader, Jim, had been serving as a beloved pastor in a large church for a number of years when he discovered that his wife of several decades had fallen in love with another man. By the time Jim found out, she had been secretly involved in the relationship for several years. As this shaken pastor talked with his most trusted friends concerning his devastating discovery, each of them exonerated him and independently recommended that he pack his wife's personal things into her suitcase, put it on the front porch and change the locks on the house. She was at fault. He was the victim. Justice now meant he should move on with his life, however he could.

He was hurt, angry, and tempted to do just that. After all, it was her sin that had destroyed their marriage. Yet, he still loved her and did not want to fracture their relationship further. Instead, he wanted to rebuild their marriage if possible. His well-meaning Christian friends easily dispensed to him an entitlement to walk away from his wife. They justified a do-over in the form of new marriage with someone different, if a fresh start was what he wanted. These well-intentioned people had bought into a grave distortion of the Christian meaning of forgiveness. Acting on their misunderstanding would almost certainly result in the dissolution of Jim's marriage. How then could Jim have heard wisdom from God concerning how to initiate a healing process with his wife so that they could start again? Would it even be possible? How could he trust his wife again? If she desired to strive with her husband to heal their marriage wounds, how could she face her friends who knew about what she had done, when their judgments condemned her? How could those who learned of the secrets of the pastor's wife forgive her of her destructive actions? After all, ministers are held to a higher standard than lay people, when it comes to the behavior of their families. Some self-righteous Christians are particularly artful at shaming others for the sins that they have not yet committed themselves. These well-intentioned friends had not grasped the historical and biblical counsel of God regarding forgiveness.

A young couple, Tom and Amy, had just returned from a final and uneventful pre-natal visit to their doctor. This baby was incredibly special to this couple. They had tried unsuccessfully to conceive a child for more than ten years. It had finally happened. Their baby daughter was full-term and would be delivered in the morning. The couple was now simply awaiting the joyous arrival of their new daughter. With no warning the young baby did not live through the night. The next day these excited parents faced both a pristine, but empty, nursery and the shocking reality of an encounter with the funeral home industry. But, insensitive friends offered well-intentioned but wounding words: "At least she is in a better place." "It was God's will to take her home." These remarks revealed that these friends had no meaningful insights into the tragedy of their suffering. How could Tom and Amy ever again experience God's immeasurable love after such great personal trauma? How could this couple forgive their church friends for their cruel comments? Even we who hear the story may be tempted to hold a grudge against God or withhold trust from God, because he does not always fix things the way we would, if we just had the power.

A dear friend, Alan, whom I had known for more than twenty-five years, had been a Christian educator for decades and positively encouraged thousands of students to know God and learn how the Christian life is about God's story, not our story. He had long dealt with two, incurable, debilitating diseases. After a lengthy and devastating battle with a third disease, he passed into the presence of God and all the historic ancient saints that he knew so well.

How can those who loved Alan and prayed ceaselessly for his healing avoid resenting God for what this good man unjustly experienced? Alan's death seemed so unfair. How do we walk through our grief and release it so that our grief does not consume us and drive us to bitterness?

I suspect that many of us identify with some of the stories recorded here. If not, then surely we have all wondered how a truly loving God allows evil people to hurt good people. Why were radical fundamentalist Muslims able to fly those planes into the World Trade Towers, that Pennsylvania field, and the Pentagon killing thousands of innocent people? Why did he permit dozens of innocent university students to be murdered on their campuses by crazy people? Hitler's atrocities were so terrible that not one of us would ever have come to his defense. After all, who could forgive him? Somehow in our rational minds there seems no room for meaningful forgiveness of evil acts committed by evil persons, especially when there is no act of contrition by the perpetrators. Following this train of thought, we are eventually tempted to pass judgment on God, who 'mistakenly' allows such terrible things to happen.

If I have voyeuristically exposed your private world of failed forgiveness, rest assured that you are not alone. You are in the company of many fellow sojourners, who face similar challenges to learn to receive and extend forgiveness in a new and more effective way—a way that provides great liberty to us and paves the way for fundamental reconciliation.

Sadly, the norm in much of our Western Christian society has become an innovative theology of conditional forgiveness. Although the axioms of innovative forgiveness are widespread and popular, they are deeply flawed. As long as we continue to view ourselves as the righteous models to follow, as long as we posture as the arbitrators of truth and dispensers of spiritual wisdom, we will never come to discern the many ancient truths about forgiveness. These truths have been revealed to us by God, through Jesus and the timeless testimony of the Scriptures. Embracing these truths is the first step toward intimacy with God and healing of our fractured relationships with God and one another. Effective spiritual formation is based on God's truth rather than our preferences.

For many years, I was unaware of the Christian spiritual formation that comes only through forgiveness. The ultimate desired result is not simply forgiveness and a life of peaceful co-existence. God desires our transformation. A transforming, redemptive process is central to the nature of God, his kingdom, and the development of Christ in us. It is to this transforming process that we now turn.

Chapter 2

The Process of Forgiveness

The Meaning of Forgiveness

The Christian theologian Dr. Catherine Dooley explains in her powerful essay on forgiveness that our foundational calling to intimacy with God and others can be restored through heart-felt forgiveness.

> Forgiveness is an intentional process in which the forgiver freely chooses not to return injury for injury but rather to respond in a loving way to the person or situation that has inflicted some harm. The process of forgiveness is not only between an individual and God or between individuals, but includes the forgiveness of self, pardon between groups and the forgiveness of social and political structures. The capacity for forgiveness generally arises out of the experience of being forgiven and leads to reconciliation or mutual acceptance. Forgiveness is a difficult process because it is unconditional.[1]

Forgiveness is one of the most controversial and misunderstood subjects in the area of religion. Dooley's explanation of forgiveness goes to the core of the Christian understanding about forgiveness. She defines forgiveness as freely choosing not to seek

---

1. Catherine Dooley, "Theology of Forgiveness" in *The New Dictionary of Sacramental Worship* (Collegeville, MN: The Liturgical Press, 1990), 473.

retribution, but instead to respond in a benevolent way to the person that has inflicted harm.

We need to be very clear when forgiveness is important and when it is not. Forgiveness is for people who have received great pain and suffering to extend to the persons that have caused them pain and suffering. Lewis Smedes states,

> Like good wine, forgiving must be preserved for the right occasion. The hurt that creates a crisis of forgiving has three dimensions. It is always *personal, unfair,* and *deep.* When you feel this kind of three-dimensional pain, you have a wound that can be healed only by forgiving the one who wounded you.[2]

We cannot forgive someone who has not hurt us.[3] Only the one who has been hurt can offer forgiveness. When our sense of hurt and pain is self-inflicted, we must extend forgiveness to ourselves. Certainly, not everything that offends us can be forgiven. Smedes' perspective on what may be forgiven is a bit narrower than what Dooley presents. Smedes argues that the concept of forgiveness is not relevant to political systems, corporate cultures, economic hardships, and unfortunate circumstances. Our anger against these things might be a great motivator for us to realign our commitments or affect positive change in those systems where we have the power to do so, but this behavior is far more about justice than forgiveness. I agree, and furthermore see no example in Jesus' teaching that references these structures as entities that should be forgiven. While Jesus does call us to rectify abuses and problems in these arenas, that teaching does not draw them within the scope of our forgiveness process, except for our forgiveness toward those individuals who directly mismanage these operations.

---

2. Lewis B. Smedes, *Forgive and Forget: Healing the Hurt We Don't Deserve* (New York: Harper Collins Publishers, 1984), 5.

3. Ibid., 5-7.

In her book *Unconditional Love and Forgiveness,* Edith R. Stauffer presents a helpful, practical explanation of what forgiveness is. She writes,

> Forgiveness can take place only within ourselves, since we are the ones whose expectations, demands, or conditions are not being met. To forgive means to cancel. What needs to be cancelled? The mental or emotional demands which we have decided must be honored in order for us to give love. Canceling is not a pardon that wipes out or restores the wrong of another. An act cannot be changed—it is a past event, a record of what happened. Canceling is neither forgetting nor the inability to remember a wrong committed. This would be impractical, as we need to remember the situation in order to protect ourselves in the future. However, we do not remember the act to use it against another; we remember it only to learn from it.[4]

The act of forgiveness requires initiation by the one who has been offended. When we have been hurt, we are the ones to forgive. This process of forgiveness is true between God and individuals as well as individuals with each other. Both Dooley and Stauffer are clear that when we are hurt, we are to offer forgiveness. As we will see later, reconciliation requires an active participation by the offending party, taking responsibility for what he or she has wrongly done, but forgiveness absolutely does not. From our examination of many Scriptures, we will see that Jesus does not require nor even suggest that the offending party plays any part in our forgiving process. The guiding principle here seems to be that when we are offended, we, who are the ones offended, are to extend forgiveness unconditionally to those who hurt us. An important perspective here is not just that Jesus commands us to do so, but that it is wise to do so, because offering forgiveness is what God has always done for all of humanity. The

---

4. Edith R. Stauffer, *Unconditional Love and Forgiveness* (Diamond Springs, CA: Triangle Publishers, 1987), 204.

capacity to extend forgiveness in this manner is an empowerment by the Spirit of God. In this sense, it is a supernatural act.

While God offers forgiveness to all, that gift of grace does not automatically restore our relationships with him without any response on our part. Rather, God's gift of forgiveness simply provides the opportunity for healing to begin. The same will be true in our human relationships—not all our relationships will be restored, even with the genuine extension of forgiveness or confession of our own inappropriate actions. Conflict resolution requires the active participation of both parties.

In his essay "Forgiveness," C. S. Lewis writes that often, instead of asking for forgiveness, he is really hoping God will excuse him. "Forgiveness says, 'Yes, you have done this thing, but I accept your apology; I will never hold it against you and everything between us two will be exactly as it was before.' But excusing says, 'I see that you couldn't help it or didn't mean it; you weren't really to blame.'"[5] If we are not to blame, then there is nothing to forgive. Forgiveness and excusing are almost opposites. Many of our actions carry some element of both. If we have a perfect excuse, we don't need forgiveness. If all of our action needs forgiveness, then there was no excuse for it. What we often call 'asking God's forgiveness' is really asking God to accept our excuses. We usually have some perceived extenuating circumstances that we must point out to God or to those we hurt. We ignore the really important thing—the part left over after the excuses are explained, but which the excuses do not cover, the portion which is inexcusable, but not, thank God, unforgivable. If we disregard this leftover part, we go away imagining that we have repented and been forgiven when all that has happened is that we have satisfied ourselves with our own excusing. They might well be very bad excuses, but we are usually too easily satisfied with ourselves.

Lewis offers two remedies for this danger. One is to acknowledge that God knows all the great excuses, even better than we do. If

_____

5. C. S. Lewis, "Forgiveness" from *The Weight of Glory* (New York, NY: HarperColllins Publishers, Inc., 2000), 178-179.

there are legitimate extenuating circumstances, we can trust that he will overlook them and we need not discuss them. What we are to take to him is the inexcusable part—the sin. The other remedy is to believe in the forgiveness of sins. Much of our emphasis on making excuses comes from not believing in forgiveness. We think that God will not take us to himself again unless he is satisfied that an effective case can be made in our favor. That action, however, would not be forgiveness. Lewis states,

> Real forgiveness means looking steadily at the sin, the sin that is left over without any excuse, after all allowances have been made, and seeing it in all its horror, dirt, meanness, and malice, and nevertheless being wholly reconciled to the man who has done it. That, and only that, is forgiveness, and that we can always have from God if we ask for it.[6]

When we forgive other people, it is partly the same, but also partly different. It is partly the same because forgiving does not mean excusing. Many people do not see the distinction. They think that if you ask them to forgive someone who has cheated them you are trying to say that there really was no cheating. But if that were so, there would be nothing to forgive. They will opine, "The man broke his promise to me." The breaking of his promise is precisely what you have to forgive. This does not mean necessarily that you must trust in his next promise. But it does mean that you will make every effort to kill every dimension of resentment—every wish to humiliate, hurt, or pay him back. What is different between this situation and the one in which we ask for God's forgiveness is that in our own case we accept our excuses too easily; in another's case, we do not accept them easily enough. But even if the offenders are unquestionably fully to blame, we still have to forgive them; and even if ninety-nine percent of his apparent guilt can be explained away with really great

---

6. Ibid, 181.

excuses, the problem of forgiveness begins with the one percent of legitimate guilt which is left over.

To excuse those actions for which there are good excuses is not Christian love, it is fairness. Christian love begins when we forgive the inexcusable part, because God has forgiven the inexcusable in us. This is not easy. It might not be too hard to forgive a single great injury, but to keep on forgiving the annoying mother-in-law, nagging wife, rude boss, or the deceitful son is extremely difficult. Lewis offers that we must mean what we say when we pray, "Forgive us our trespasses as we forgive those who trespass against us." We are not offered forgiveness on any other terms. To refuse to forgive others is to refuse God's mercy for ourselves. God offers no hint of exceptions to what he says.

Forgiving others is not some disciplined 'repression' but a change of heart. It is a change in the way we see harmful events and harmful people. One of the key elements of forgiveness is unleashing the redemptive story of God upon ourselves and others. We learn to retell or 'reframe' the human drama through the redemptive lens of Christ and his work. This perspective is what ultimately gives meaning to human history. Through this reframing process, our hearts are changed from within and our love for the other person grows, despite what he or she has done. The provision of forgiveness is a sure anchor for Christians in the storms of relationships.

Joseph's Practice of Unconditional Forgiveness

An early example of unconditional forgiveness recorded in Scripture was that offered by Joseph to his brothers. Genesis, chapters 37-50, records the traumas inflicted upon Joseph, who was only seventeen at the time, by his brothers. They plotted to kill him because they were jealous of the favor shown to Joseph by their father, Jacob. When the opportunity presented itself, they sold him into slavery. Joseph was taken to Egypt, several hundred miles from the land of the Hebrews where his family lived. His brothers then led their father to believe that he was dead. The loss of Joseph broke Jacob's heart. Years passed during which God provided for Joseph in Egypt. He was eventually appointed by Pharaoh to oversee the entire land of Egypt.[7] When a terrible famine occurred in the land of the Hebrews, Joseph's brothers traveled to Egypt to purchase grain. They encountered Joseph, but did not know him, though Joseph recognized them instantly. Through a complicated and dramatic chain of events, Joseph eventually revealed to them that he was their brother whom they had sold into slavery. Naturally, they were very fearful that he might put them to death, because he was now a powerful man. Instead, Joseph told his brothers, "do not be distressed and do not be angry with yourselves for selling me here, because it was to save lives that God sent me ahead of you" (Gen 45:5). He continued his loving response to his brothers not only by giving them food but also by bringing them, their families, and their father down to Egypt. In this way, Joseph saved them all from starvation, because the famine continued for several more years.

Certainly, Joseph's brothers had dealt him a great life tragedy. Fortunately, Joseph's frame of reference was not his own self-interest, but God's point of view. Joseph had become a theocentric thinker. This enabled him not only to forgive his brothers for their cruelty and selfishness, but moved him beyond forgiveness to bless them and their families. Joseph did not simply 'decide' to forgive his brothers. Rather, because of who he had become and because he knew God, his worldview had been transformed.

The lens through which we view the world will determine how we extend forgiveness to others and whether or not we feel retribution is appropriate. If we view our nation and our possessions as our own property or expect our relationships to be endowed with certain entitlements, then we are primarily driven by our own self-interests. Because Joseph viewed himself and all around him as belonging to God, his way of *being* was to forgive and extend love to

---

7. See Gen 41:41.

his brothers. His radical, God-centered perspective *freed* Joseph to love the brothers who had caused him so much pain.

God's Gift of Forgiveness

If we are to emulate Joseph, our human experience of forgiveness must become rooted in the reality of forgiveness offered to us by God. God has shown us his ongoing mercy throughout antiquity in the Judeo-Christian writings. We read of one such example in the recorded history of Israel's exodus from Egypt. After Moses had led the Israelites in the desert for some time, he went up on Mt. Sinai to be with God and receive the stone tablets on which God had inscribed his Ten Commandments. While Moses was with God, his brother Aaron instructed the Israelites to collect their gold jewelry. He melted the gold and made an idol in the shape of a calf.[8] God knew what was happening, was very angry, and yet still forgave them. Over the years, despite the Israelites' ongoing sins, God continued to be merciful to them. In the wilderness, God drew his people to himself during their travels by meeting with them in the tabernacle. He dwelled with them in the Ark of the Covenant within the first temple in Jerusalem. Through it all, God repeatedly initiated relationships with his people and explicitly revealed his process for their forgiveness, which involved a sacrificial system of worship.

Another example of forgiveness was much later than Moses but still hundreds of years before the birth of Jesus. The Psalmist proclaims, "Blessed are those whose transgressions are forgiven, whose sins are covered. Blessed are those whose sin the Lord does not count against him and in whose spirit is no deceit.... I said, 'I will confess my transgressions to the Lord'—and you forgave the guilt of my sin" (Psalm 32:1, 2, 5). We see, here, not only God's part of the forgiveness process, but also the offender's part. In addition to sacrifice, the human side of forgiveness included the act of confession. A person was to confess his or her sins and, at the same time, have no deceit

---

8. See Exod 32-34.

about it, whether before God or anyone else. One is deceitful within one's spirit when an attempt is made to convince others that one is following God when he or she is actually choosing not to do so. Most of us quickly spot such hypocritical behavior in others while we often miss it in ourselves.

The sacrificial system for forgiveness continued for well over a thousand years. Since the original event, countless generations of Jews have celebrated the Passover to remind them of God's provision and protection during their escape from Egypt. The early Christians viewed the sacrificial history of the Passover as the context into which God sent his Son to be the ultimate innocent sacrifice.[9] Another widely held perspective in the early Church asserted that through the cross and resurrection, Jesus won a cosmic victory over death and the demonic forces of evil, which torment humans.[10] Christian theologians differ on whether the fundamental nature of the atonement is sacrificial, substitutionary, or cosmic. But all three perspectives are in harmony with the fundamental conviction that God's Son offered to come and be in our midst and to be sacrificed so that we could have a restored and renewed relationship with God. All who trust in him enter into a relationship with God.

Jesus understood forgiveness perfectly. On the night that he was betrayed to the temple guards, Jesus celebrated the Passover dinner with his twelve disciples. He was still lovingly in communion with all his disciples—even Judas, the one that he knew would identify him for thirty pieces of silver. The money was likely already in Judas's pocket, since Judas had already made his contract with the established religious leaders prior to the dinner that evening. Even with the knowledge of his eminent betrayal and death, Jesus exhibited

---

9. This is the very prominent theology of penal substitutionary atonement, whereby Jesus' death satisfies the wrath of God against sin. The sacrificial death of his Son is substituted for our eternal punishment.

10. This theory of the atonement is called *Christus Victor,* or Christ the Victor. It is rooted in the Incarnation and the conviction that Jesus came to win the final victory over sin and the destructive forces that hold humanity in subjection.

a profound level of pre-forgiveness. Knowing what his future held, he did not reject the one who would betray him. These are the words he spoke that night:

> And he took bread, gave thanks and broke it, and gave it to them, saying, "This is my body given for you; do this in remembrance of me." In the same way, after the supper he took the cup, saying, "This cup is the new covenant in my blood, which is poured out for you. But the hand of him who is going to betray me is with mine on the table. The Son of Man will go as it has been decreed, but woe to that man who betrays him." They began to question among themselves which of them it might be who would do this. (Luke 22:19-23)

What the reader often overlooks in this passage is the completely unambiguous verb 'given'. Jesus' life was not taken from him. The obedient act of Jesus' giving of himself was probably the most loving and far-reaching act that anyone could initiate. The first Christian theologians quoted the prophet Isaiah in chapter 53 in regards to Jesus, "The Lord has laid on him the iniquity of us all" (v. 6b), "Yet, it was the Lord's will to crush him and cause him to suffer" (v. 10), and "He poured out his life unto death, and was numbered with the transgressors. For he bore the sin of many, and made intercession for the transgressors" (v. 12). At this supper Jesus was not only celebrating the Passover and the way in which God had faithfully provided for his chosen people in the past, but he also was celebrating what he knew to be the ultimate demonstration of God's faithfulness. When he gave his followers bread at the last supper, he gave them not only food for their bodies but nourishment for their souls as well. He then explained to them that the gift of the bread and wine was to continually remind them of the life-giving forgiveness that he provided for them through the offering of his life. The word that is translated 'remembrance'[11] has a meaning in the biblical language that is difficult to translate into English. It means much more than recalling a

---

11. The Greek word used in the gospels is *anamnesis*.

historic fact. The meaning Jesus was conveying was that the signifi-cance of the historic act of the giving of his life for us at that point in history is to impact us in the present moment, providing us with an ongoing relationship with him in the present.

By giving his life, Jesus provides a way for all who accept God's provision to enter into a relationship with God. Forgiveness, then, is about connection. Because we are forgiven, we can be connected to ourselves, God, to the nature of Christ, and to other people. Forgive-ness opens the channel for the sustenance necessary for life. Without God's forgiveness, we are disconnected from God. If we withhold forgiveness from one another, then we can receive no sustenance from one another because we are disconnected. Where forgiveness is given or received, restoration can be anticipated. Wounds—endured and inflicted—can be healed.

From the cross, Jesus prayed to his Father on behalf of those who were crucifying him, "Father, forgive them, for they do not know what they are doing" (Luke 23: 34). In our culture we tend to excuse wrong behavior when it is done out of ignorance. Jesus does not. It was because ignorance was no excuse that Jesus asked his Father to forgive them even though they were continuing to inflict fatal cru-elty upon him. We can infer that because Jesus interceded on their behalf, that he had forgiven them. This petition for mercy shows us his unconditional love for those who were perpetrating the greatest violence against him. Once again Jesus showed us that the exten-sion of forgiveness is never contingent in any way upon some action on the part of the offender. His exhibition of forgiveness was made with the clear understanding that the soldiers did not know the sig-nificance of their actions. Certainly, they knew that he was about to die, but they had no idea what would follow as a result. They did not know who Jesus really was (and is), God in human form. Many assumed he was a justly condemned criminal. While he was suffer-ing, Jesus forgave all those who were putting him to death with their own hands. Jesus offers us forgiveness on the same terms.

The gospel of John records Jesus saying, "I am the way and the truth and the life. No one comes to the Father except through me. If you really know me, you will know my Father as well. From now on, you do know him and have seen him" (John 14:6). The phrase 'through me' means *by way of*, as in what happens when we walk through a doorway from one place into another.

Some have attempted to revise the meaning of this passage implying that we are to come to God as Jesus came to God. In this view Jesus is believed to have been embraced by God for his faithfulness and subsequently became God-like. This makes no sense in light of the conviction of the first apostles that Jesus was God in the flesh. Following his resurrection, when Jesus showed Thomas his wounded hands and his side that had been pierced, Thomas exclaimed, "My Lord and my God" (John 20:28b). John also wrote, "In the beginning was the Word, and the Word was with God, and the Word was God. He [Jesus] was with God in the beginning. Through him [Jesus] all things were made; without him nothing was made that has been made" (John 1:1-3). Jesus did not 'become' God at some midpoint of his life; he is not a model for our coming to God, but the God to whom we are to come.

The apostle Peter was addressing Jews in Jerusalem and declared to them that God had made Jesus, whom they had crucified, both Lord and Christ.[12] These were two distinct, bold declarations to the Jews there. Identifying Jesus as Lord acknowledged that Yahweh had declared that Jesus was to be respected, one who has power or authority.[13] 'Christ' is the English word for the Greek *Christos*, 'anointed one'. The Hebrew word for this person is *Mashiach*, that is, Messiah.[14] Thus, Peter declared that God had announced Jesus to be the Messiah. Both of these declarations put Jews in attendance into

---

12. See Acts 2:36.

13. Chad Brand, Charles Draper, Archie England, General Editors, "Lord" in the *Holman Illustrated Bible Dictionary* (Nashville, TN: Holman Bible Publishers, 2003), 1046-1047.

14. Ibid., 284.

a crisis. As a result several Jews desired to respond to God's loving provision of Jesus, whom they had seen crucified. When they asked what they should do, Peter boldly replied, "Repent and be baptized, every one of you, in the name of Jesus Christ for the forgiveness of your sins. And you will receive the gift of the Holy Spirit" (Acts 2:38). As we see our sin, we must acknowledge it and turn away from our destructive behavior without hesitation. Sin is not destructive simply because it is ill-advised, self-centered, or even because it inflicts pain upon others, though all of these consequences are damaging. It is destructive primarily because it is contrary to God's point of view. It diminishes or destroys that which God created and loves. We look to God only through Jesus Christ for our forgiveness. That the gift of divine forgiveness is available only through Jesus Christ is unequivocally central to the Christian faith. This process by which we receive it was designed by God the Father and is carried out by God the Son.

We have no historical or biblical basis to operate otherwise, no matter how challenging we might find these declarations. In fact, the ancient church strongly refuted all challenges to this standard. Athanasius (c. 293–373 A.D.), the Bishop of Alexandria (Egypt) and a prominent leader in the ancient church was a major player in the refutation of the Arian theology that was emerging in his day. The followers of another bishop, Arius, depicted Christ as a created being, rather than God enfleshed. In various persuasive writings[15] Athanasius refuted Arius, strongly affirming that God's son was present with the Father from the beginning of time. Athanasius argued that because Jesus is God incarnate and fully divine he is able to save and redeem humanity.

Jesus' bold assertion that one comes to God exclusively through him is reaffirmed by the apostle Peter who declared to the Jewish rulers and elders that salvation is found through no one other

---

15. See "On the Incarnation" and "Against the Arians" by Athanasius.

than Jesus Christ of Nazareth, who was crucified and raised from the dead.[16] On this point the ancient church was absolutely immovable.

In John 14:6 above, Jesus claims to be the truth. Knowing truth is to know reality—not just the facts about reality. Truth is actualized in the person of Jesus Christ. William Temple, the Archbishop of Canterbury in the mid-twentieth century, writes of Jesus that:

> We have to pass through Him if we are to come to
> the Father; we must be so united with Him that as
> He offers Himself to the Father He offers us also.
> …If the Gospel is true, and God is, as the Bible de-
> clares, a Living God, the ultimate truth is not a system
> of propositions grasped by perfect intelligence, but is a
> Personal Being apprehended in the only way in which
> persons are ever fully apprehended, that is, by love.
> The Incarnation is not condescension to our infirmi-
> ties, so that "Truth embodied in a tale" may enter in
> the "lowly door" of human minds. It is the only way
> in which divine truth can be expressed, not because
> of our infirmity but because of its own nature. What
> is personal can be expressed only in a person.[17]

Throughout his earthly ministry, Jesus Christ repeatedly taught his followers about the critical need for forgiveness and reconciliation between God and humankind as well as one human and another. The apostle Paul explained to the Ephesians how God initiated this blessing and extended forgiveness to us as a gift.

> But because of his great love for us, God, who is
> rich in mercy, made us alive with Christ even when
> we were dead in transgression—it is by grace you
> have been saved. And God raised us up with Christ
> and seated us with him in the heavenly realms in

---

16. See Acts 4:8-12 where Peter and John were teaching before the Sanhedrin, the high religious leaders of the Jews. It was in essence their Supreme Court of ancient Israel. This teaching was not well received by them.

17. William Temple, *Readings in St. John's Gospel* (London: Macmillan and Co., Limited, 1952), 230-231.

Christ Jesus, in order that in the coming ages he might show the incomparable riches of his grace, expressed in his kindness to us in Christ Jesus. For it is by grace you have been saved, through faith—and this is not from yourselves, it is the gift of God—not by works, so that no one can boast. (Eph 2:4-9)

Of particular interest are the antecedents of the words 'this' and 'it' in the last sentence of the passage. Does the gift of God refer to salvation or does the gift include faith? Saint John Chrysostom (c. 347-407 A.D.), the Archbishop of Constantinople, taught that we could do nothing to earn salvation, but that salvation and our faith are both gifts from God. Some persons might argue that faith is our responsibility and work, but Chrysostom argues that had Jesus not come, had he not called us, how could we have been able to believe? Therefore, the work of faith itself is not our own; it is a gift to us from God.[18]

God's forgiveness cannot be earned. One cannot earn a gift. God's offer of forgiveness was made to us without requiring anything of us first. As Scripture states, "But God demonstrates his own love for us in this: While we were still sinners, Christ died for us" (Rom 5:8). Jesus offered himself on our behalf not because we were good and we deserved it, but because we were not good and needed it. Our response to his love is our love for him and for others. "We love because he first loved us" (1 John 4:19). John 3:16 states in part, "For God so loved the world that he gave his one and only Son." God's love for us was not simply a feeling of affection. It was rooted in his willingness to make a supreme sacrifice for those whom he loved. Because he loved, he gave. His love and his giving were quite costly. God's offer of forgiveness is unconditional and it is completely at his initiation. Despite Jesus Christ's prayer to his father that he be spared

18. St. John Chrysostom, "Homily IV, Homilies on Ephesians" from *Nicene and Post-Nicene Fathers of the Christian Church, First Series,* vol. XIII, Philip Schaff, ed. (Grand Rapids, MI: Wm. B. Eerdmans Publishing Company, 1970), 67.

the agony of the cross,[19] he voluntarily died for us while we lived in sin, because he loved us and was obedient to his Father.[20] Jesus did not desire to die; yet he chose to die. When teaching the Pharisees, Jesus told them, "The reason my Father loves me is that I lay down my life—only to take it up again. No one takes it from me, but I lay it down of my own accord. I have authority to lay it down and authority to take it up again. This command I received from my Father" (John 10:17-18). Because of Jesus' love for humanity, he complied with his Father's request. Neither the original disciples nor we are in any way responsible for Jesus' voluntary decision to sacrifice himself on our behalf. We are, however, the recipients of the benefits of his sacrifice, if we accept his gift.

When we strive to be forgiven by God, we must be careful not to resurrect an ancient church heresy called adoptionism. Adoptionism suggested that Jesus was adopted into divinity, rather than being God enfleshed from his birth. The theory goes that perhaps Jesus became God at his baptism, as a reward for his good life. Such thinking about Jesus promotes the fantasy that we, too, can be adopted into God's family based on our exemplary actions instead of on the gift from God. If we attribute our forgiveness as coming about through the merits of our own virtues, the need for Jesus' sacrifice is eliminated. Today, derivatives of this destructive theology are often found where conformity to moral legalism becomes the litmus test of whether or not someone is a Christian. Before welcoming someone new into a church, some people might ask, "Do they refrain from certain practices or do they conform to other specific unacceptable lifestyles?" Each of us could probably prepare a list of potential spiritual barometers by polling or observing our own Christian community. Employing such litmus tests promotes the inflation of our own egos, when we mistakenly believe that God has aligned his perspective with ours. Unquestionably, a Christian is to exhibit a high moral character and ethical behavior, but precisely

---

19. See Isa 53.
20. See Matt 26:42.

where we draw the line is what is in question. Is it that others know, love, and follow Jesus or do we require them to tithe to the church and abstain from drinking a glass of wine?

In our process of Christian conversion, we are called to respond to God, overcome pride, and forgive others just as we have been forgiven, but not because we have somehow earned forgiveness. Theologian James Torrance makes clear that "God accepts us, not because of our repentance—we have no worthy penitence to offer—but in the person of one [Jesus Christ] who has already said amen for us, in death, to the divine condemnation of our sin—in atonement."[21] Our life of worship of God and countless other good deeds are not things that we do to counterbalance our sins and thereby bring us into favor with God resulting in our forgiveness. Jesus' sacrifice is the only sacrifice acceptable to God for the forgiveness of our sins. In the Epistle to the Hebrews the author makes it clear that only the blood and death of Jesus removes sin and makes it possible for sinners to draw near to God.[22] Because Jesus offered himself as a perfectly obedient and unblemished sacrifice to his father, Jesus' death has atoning significance.[23] To atone means to reconcile or to bring together of two persons, who have formerly been enemies, into a relationship of peace and friendship. The Hebrew root of atonement, *kaphar,* means to cover. Just as pitch [tar] covered the ancient ark built by Noah and protected its passengers, so the sacrificially shed blood of Jesus stands between humankind and the holy God.[24] With a single sacrifice for sins, Christ has removed the necessity for the previous old covenant sacrificial system, providing the final and decisive forgiveness of which the prophet Jeremiah spoke.[25]

---

21. James B. Torrance, *Worship, Community & the Triune God of Grace* (Downers Grove, IL: InterVarsity Press, 1996), 56. Parenthetical insertion by the author.

22. See Heb 9:12-14, 15-22, 10:19, 29, 12:24, 13:12.

23. See Heb 5:7-9, 7:27, 9:14, 28.

24. Merrill C. Tenney, ed., "Atonement" in *The Zondervan Pictorial Bible Dictionary* (Grand Rapids, MI: Zondervan Publishing House, 1971), 83.

25. Jer 10:17-18. Also see David Peterson, *Engaging with God* (Downers Grove, IL: InterVarsity Press, 1992), 231-232.

Thus, according to the teachings of Scripture, Jesus' sacrifice is not only sufficient, but also the exclusive means by which we are made right with God.[26] As I stated earlier, the ancient church was adamant on this issue.

---

26. Heb 10:10, Heb 5:8-10, John 14:6.

Chapter 3
Receiving and Extending Forgiveness

Responding to God's Forgiveness

Forgiveness in religious cultures is sometimes a programmed activity. For example, in many churches today there is a belief that the church, the authorized clergy, or the proper performance of a religious ritual itself somehow bestows God's forgiveness to individuals. God has no proxies. In the ancient church neither baptism nor participation in the Eucharist[1] was the formula for receiving God's forgiveness. Sacraments were not magical events performed by a special class of Christians. Sacraments were affirmations by the individual and the body of Christ of what God had done, was doing, and would be doing in them individually and also within the Christian community.

In the first years of Christianity, new converts were baptized immediately upon their acceptance and response to the gift of salvation offered through Christ. Over the years, however, the process of incorporation was rescripted. The first Christians had been life-long Jews. They believed in one just and merciful God rather than many capricious gods. Their Jewish heritage provided a very solid basis

---

1. *Eucharistia* is a Greek word used in the New Testament Scripture that literally means 'thanksgiving'. In the first centuries of the Christian church, *Eucharist* became the name for the observance of the last supper Jesus shared with his disciples before his betrayal and death. It was partaken with great thanksgiving to God for his sacrificial love and the gift of salvation. The practice later became known as Communion or the Lord's Supper by many Protestant Christians.

from which to learn about and then embrace Jesus as the Messiah. As the gospel was carried into the Hellenistic (Greek) world, new gentile converts had no historical foundation on which to understand God. Consequently, Gnostic teaching and other emerging heresies threatened the churches. The general lack of knowledge called for new converts to receive formational and life-changing education and assessment to help them become well-grounded in their new faith. Church leaders eventually implemented a specific plan of instruction and assessment for those seeking to become a part of the church.

Hippolytus is credited with writing the *Apostolic Tradition* soon after his accession as the Bishop of Rome in A.D. 217. In this historic document he affirmed many practices that had been long-established within Christian churches for as many as fifty years prior to his writings. Articles XX 1 and 2 were written about those who were to receive baptism. These state,

> And when they are chosen who are set apart to re-
> ceive baptism, let their life be examined, whether
> they lived piously while catechumens[2], whether
> 'they honoured the widows', whether they visited the
> sick, whether they have fulfilled every good work.
> If those who bring them bear witness to them that
> have done this, then let them hear the gospel. [3]

These instructions explicitly state that only the believers who exhibited a life above reproach with generous love and compassion for others would be baptized. One did not *decide* to be baptized; rather he or she was *chosen*, sponsored by someone already baptized, and the candidate must have fulfilled "every good work." Here Hippolytus was speaking of reflecting God's character in our lifestyle,

---

2. A catechumen was a person who had asked to receive instruction in the ways of God and who had initially accepted the gift of salvation through Jesus Christ. Catechumens were engaged in a learning process that would eventually result in their being baptized at some point in the future when they had grown stronger in their faith and Godly character.

3. Gregory Dix, *The Apostolic Tradition of St. Hippolytus* (London: Society for Promoting Christian Knowledge, 1937), xxxv.

not being perfect in all areas of one's life. At this point the Christians faced the possibility of death at the hands of the government because of their affirmation of Christ at baptism. The very fact that Christians would secretly worship together despite the risk of death meant that there was an astonishing level of trust. They did not want their mutual trust and unity compromised. Hippolytus does not give specific details of reconciliation between conflicted Christians, but we may infer that anyone not living in right relationship with his brothers and sisters would not be admitted for baptism until a pious character was demonstrated and acknowledged by the sponsor for baptism.

As many as three years of instruction and satisfactory assessment were required by church leaders before catechumens were admitted to baptism and only thereafter were they welcomed to the Eucharist. The ancient churches discerned that this lengthy time was necessary to confidently establish that a person had truly accepted the grace of God. It also provided the new Christians enough time to experience conflict and resolution in the community.

Eventually, the churches developed formal rites (or rituals) commemorating their forgiveness with baptism. Although church instruction about forgiveness and baptism can be programmed, forgiveness, itself, never is. The writings of Hippolytus and another text called *The Didache*, discussed later, both deal with instructions about baptism which was regarded as the principal symbol for reconciliation with God. Baptism also recognized that a person was drawn into the Christian community, had decided to follow Christ and learn of him, made a public affirmation of their allegiance to God, and had been acknowledged by a Christian sponsor as a person of faith and strong character. In this understanding, baptism is not simply the moment one is touched by the baptismal waters, but is the highlight of initial Christian formation.

Our appropriate response to God for what he has done in forgiving us is a heart full of humble gratitude. Otherwise, we are apt to believe we have permission to sit in judgment of others. It is only as we personally come to grips with the mercy of God that we are able to cease believing that we are somehow better or more deserving than others. Only as we see our own sin and experience the love from God that he offers us, can we defuse our hostility and arrogance toward those who hurt us. Awareness of God's forgiveness calls us to live very differently from our secular friends. Not only are we full of gratitude and thanksgiving, but we also embrace confession, repentance, and the experience of reconciliation.

God offers us all many moments of grace and forgiveness along the way. In these moments, we may move toward God as he offers forgiveness or we may choose to ignore him. Refusing to restore a broken relationship with God ultimately determines our own destiny with God, but as we move toward God we also learn how to love and forgive others.

When we have received God's forgiveness, we have a model for how to receive it from and extend it to others. If we are privileged to receive forgiveness from someone who we have hurt, then our response to him or her should be the same response we give to God. We express our genuine thanks for their forgiveness. Our response is not merely pronouncement of thanks, but a fitting culmination of appropriate confession and repentance. We can then enjoy the blessing of being reconciled with our estranged friend or enemy.

Our Forgiveness Choices about Others

Many Christian teachers announce that we simply must forgive those who hurt us, saying it is a choice we must make. But it actually involves a series of choices. Once we choose to forgive the person, we must then make choices about how we will now relate to that person. We must change our attitude of disappointment by canceling expectations that we have held in the past. The most significant choice we face is whether or not we will love the person. Forgiveness is not an end in itself. Forgiveness is a means of expressing love in the world. Forgiving because we love is very different from love that is *quid pro quo*—responding in love because we are receiving love. If we 'forgive' someone but still avoid being around them and continue to maintain a 'righteous' judgment of them, we delude ourselves. We have not forgiven them. If we are uncertain whether we have truly forgiven someone, an indicator of our heart might be whether we will pray for God to bless the one who has hurt us. When we can ask God to bless them we have passed through the process of forgiveness and arrived at love.

The writer of Proverbs informs us that "a person's wisdom yields patience; it is to one's glory to overlook an offense" (Proverbs 19:11). It is the nature of a transformed person to respond to evil with good. When we can simply overlook an offense with no need for judgment or retaliation, we make a choice that exhibits the wisdom of restraint and patience.

In the Sermon on the Mount Jesus said, "You have heard it was said, 'Love your neighbor and hate your enemy.' But I tell you, love your enemies and pray for those who persecute you, that you may be children of your Father in heaven" (Matt 5:43-45). Do not misread the purpose of our prayers for our enemies. Note that Jesus said we are to pray for them so that *we* will be children of our heavenly Father—not so that *they* will become children of our heavenly Father. What do you suppose we are to pray for these enemies? Jesus does not elaborate. We are tempted to say imprecatory prayers[4], but this is probably not what Jesus had in mind! Instead, prayers could certainly include their coming to know God as well as other blessings that seem suitable.

In the Sermon on the Mount Jesus taught, "Blessed are the peacemakers, for they will be called the sons of God" (Matt 5:9). Christians are to be peaceable. We are to strive to live in harmony with others and when we come into conflict, help one another work

---

4. Imprecatory prayers are those in which one asks either for the demise of opponents or for evil to overtake and afflict them. There are such prayers in the Psalms and they can be considered troublesome to those who do not understand the process of lamenting.

through it. He continues with, "Settle matters quickly with your adversary who is taking you to court" (Matt 5:25). Here, he is exhorting someone who has failed at some legal obligation toward another person. We are to quickly work out solutions to our disputes, especially if we are the one causing the problem. These exhortations encourage Jesus' listeners to seek a solution of peacefully moving forward, before they face having the court make the decision for both of them.

It is a challenge to remain loving toward someone who is hurting us. We may try to explain away their behavior, but we are still hurting. Those who hurt us might be striking at us out of their own pain or they might unconsciously perceive in us, rightly or wrongly, a quality or trait of their own of which they do not approve. Whether or not we understand their motives, forgiving them is the one thing we can do to create the possibility of well-being and peace. We are to cultivate a loving heart and extend forgiveness without regard for the condition of the heart of the one we are forgiving. This is the same way God forgives.

Jesus taught his disciples to pray, "Forgive us our sins, for we also forgive everyone who sins against us. And lead us not into temptation" (Luke 11:4). Jesus' words do not seem to leave much maneuvering room. We are asked by Jesus to pray to God asking for our own forgiveness, affirming that we have forgiven everyone who sins against us—*everyone!*—remorseful or not.

Interestingly, Jesus used only plural pronouns in his model prayer. This implies a community wherein confession and forgiveness are part of an ongoing way of life. Relationships in such a community would be unconditional, rather than conditional, selected relationships. Forgiving others in this context would not be a one-time event, but an ongoing process that is inseparable from seeking forgiveness for our own actions before God and other people.

Furthermore, Jesus links God's forgiveness of us to our willingness to forgive others. In Matthew's version of Jesus' model prayer, Jesus speaks clearly: "For if you forgive others when they sin against you, your heavenly Father will also forgive you. But if you do not forgive others their sins, your Father will not forgive your sins" (Matt 6:14-15). Jesus is saying that our unwillingness to forgive those who have hurt us will preclude our receiving forgiveness for our own sins. There is no doubt about it; if we do not forgive those who hurt us, Jesus says that God will not forgive our sins.

In a letter to the church at Colossae, the apostle Paul encouraged followers of Christ to forgive in the same way God forgives. He wrote,

> Therefore, as God's chosen people, holy and dearly
> loved, clothe yourselves with compassion, kindness,
> humility, gentleness, and patience. Bear with each
> other and forgive one another if any of you has a griev-
> ance against one another. Forgive as the Lord forgave
> you. And over all these virtues put on love, which
> binds them all together in perfect unity. (Col 3:12-13)

Here, Paul does not say to forgive because God has forgiven you, (although he does elsewhere to encourage us to forgive others), but says, instead, to forgive *as,* that is, *in the same manner that* God forgives. God, in Christ, forgave unconditionally, even as he was being executed. The point here is that we are to initiate unconditional offers of forgiveness to others.

Paul broadens the scope of forgiveness even further when he writes to the Christians in Rome, "If it is possible, as far as it depends upon you, live at peace with everyone. Do not take revenge" (Rom 12:18-29a). Here, Paul concedes that not all broken relationships will be reestablished. Nevertheless, our agenda must be to forgive and never be the obstinate one who stands in the way of reconciliation. The Christian is to be the redemptive influence upon the relationship, never the one who withdraws or refuses to strive toward rebuilding the relationship. Forgiving others is absolutely necessary, never optional, and must not be conditional. These tough words about forgiveness from Jesus' Sermon on the Mount, reinforced by the apostle Paul, probably seem quite unusual to us and meet with considerable resistance in our culture. These teachings are not promoted by some contemporary Bible teachers, because this message about giving unconditional forgiveness is unlikely to appeal to anyone living out of a strong sense of individual autonomy or a passion for policing their personal rights. But the biblical accounts of forgiveness focus on people who, in the context of community, passionately pursue a relationship with God and relational healing of others.

In the chapter that follows, we will explore the truths unearthed thus far in greater depth, as we seek to describe the essential characteristics of people for whom the giving and receiving of forgiveness are both a means of grace and a proof to the world that we have received it.

Chapter 4

The Characteristics of Forgiveness

Forgiveness Is Loving

The gospel message teaches everywhere that we are to seek and extend forgiveness out of love. Jesus himself made love the foundation of all Christian obedience, when he said,

> "Love the Lord your God with all your heart and with all your soul and all your mind." This is the first and the greatest commandment. And the second is like it: "Love your neighbor as yourself." All the Law and the Prophets hang on these two commandments. (Matt 22:37-40)

The apostle John declares, "God is love" (1 John 4:16). Love is central to God's nature and, therefore, John warns, "If we say we love God yet hate a brother or sister, we are liars. For if we do not love a fellow believer, whom we have seen, we cannot love God, whom we have not seen. And he has given us this command: Those who love God must also love one another" (1 John 4:20-21).

The apostle Paul counseled the Christians in the church at Ephesus to "be kind and compassionate to one another, forgiving each other, just as in Christ God forgave you" (Eph 4:32). The imperative, here, is for Christians to initiate forgiveness toward all others as we gratefully remember how God has initiated with us. To the Christians in Rome, Paul wrote, "But God demonstrates his own love for us in this: While we were still sinners, Christ died for us" (Rom 5:8). Just as Christ died for us before we could change or even show remorse, we are to love those who have offended us. Contrary to our natural human preference, forgiveness is not offered as a response to any actions—or lack thereof—on the part of anyone else.

The nature of the Christian is to be conformed to the nature of God. Forgiving one another is to be central to our character, just as it is to God's character. We forgive people we love. When we do not love, we do not forgive.

In Greek, the verb we translate as 'love' in these passages of Scripture is *agape*.[1] This love is not the brotherly love of tender affection (*phileo*)[2] or the love that acquires something for one's self (*eros*). Instead, *agape* is the self-giving type of love. Speaking of *agape*, theologians W. Günther and H. G. Link state that it means to treat respectfully, to be pleased with and to welcome. It is a generous move by one for the sake of the other.[3] In the famous 'Love Chapter', the apostle Paul describes *agape* in profoundly practical terms. "Love is patient, love is kind. It does not envy, it does not boast, it is not proud. It does not dishonor others [is not rude], it keeps no record of wrongs" (1 Cor 13:4-5). It can only be known by the actions it prompts.[4]

Although this passage is often quoted at marriage ceremonies, Paul is not just describing love within the family. This type of love describes the attitude of God toward his Son (John 17:26) and the human race collectively (John 17:26 and Rom 5:8). *Agape* is not an impulse from feelings or natural inclinations, nor is it extended

---

1. John Schwandt, ed., *The English-Greek Reverse Interlinear New Testament* (Wheaton, IL: Crossway Books, 2006), 23.

2. These three nuances of the meaning of love are not to be understood as mutually exclusive. Mature Christians experience all three types of love. Describing the affection that the Father has for the Son, in John 5:20, the apostle uses the form *phileo*. This gives us an even more broad understanding of the nature of God's love, noting that it is both affectionate as well as self-giving.

3. Colin Brown, ed., "Love" by W. Günther and H. G. Link from the *New International Dictionary of New Testament Theology*, vol. 2 (Grand Rapids, MI: Zondervan, 1986), 539.

4. W. E. Vine, "Love" in *Vine's Expository Dictionary of Old and New Testament Words*, vol. 3 (Old Tappan, NJ: Fleming H. Revell Company, 1981), 21.

only toward those with whom one shares some affinity. Jesus made this meaning clear when he said, "Love your enemies and pray for those who persecute you" (Matt 5:44-45).

This is the love that emanates from the heart of God and the type of love he desires to cultivate in us. God's love seeks the welfare of everyone and brings no ill to anyone. When our innermost self generates this kind of love we move ahead in our experience of spiritual formation.

We must not, however, confuse forgiving in *agape* love with being 'nice' to people who have unjustly hurt us or those we love while, inside, we burn with resentment and bitterness. Loving even our enemies, as Jesus taught, is not a call to masochistically 'grin and bear it'. Some of us are quite skillful at ostensibly shutting down our emotions, especially when they take us to places where we are no longer in control. We numb ourselves to the loss of the joy we might still have with those who have broken our hearts. Powerful psychological forces such as fear of rejection or wrongly embedded Christian teaching may well impel us to regulate our outward behavior, yet bring almost no resolution to our real internal conflicts. Much of what we call stress could be a symptom of masked unforgiveness of others or our own refusal to accept God's forgiveness on the terms he establishes. We might will ourselves to forgive outwardly, only to discover that we are then held hostage by this counterfeit of forgiveness, which cannot bring healing to our hurting relationships.

Only as we experience God enabling us to love, do we become free to forgive. When we receive a new vision of the great love that God has extended to us, we can begin in response to tender an *agape*—a selfless love—to those who have hurt us. Forgiveness of others, when it is genuine, will help dissipate the grief and stress that comes from being wounded and from losing relationships with those we love. Our loving initiative of forgiveness opens the door for the forgiven ones to safely approach us. Forgiveness is the necessary first step in the process by which one can renew love and trust.

Forgiveness Is to Be Ongoing

Ideally, we would enjoy long-term relationships where the bond of love is never severed. But in the reality of life, the best of relationships suffer conflict, misunderstandings and, from time to time, even destructive behaviors that break relationships. In the first epistle of John, clearly written to Christians, not non-Christians, this is certainly true, at least from our side, in our relationship with God: "If we claim to be without sin, we deceive ourselves and the truth is not in us. If we confess our sins, he is faithful and just and will forgive us our sins and purify us from all unrighteousness" (1 John 1:2-10). Christians still commit sins and, therefore, are in need of ongoing forgiveness and restoration.

Just as ongoing forgiveness from God is necessary, so it is in personal relationships. In Matthew 18, a lengthy discourse on forgiveness to which we will return, Jesus makes clear how important it is when Peter asks, "Lord, how many times shall I forgive my brother when he sins against me? Up to seven times?" The Jewish leaders of the time believed in forgiveness, but taught that one must forgive three times and then draw the line at forgiving the offender on the fourth or subsequent occasions. With this question, Peter pushed forgiveness to a new level of graciousness by suggesting seven times; this level would be more than twice that required by the Jewish leaders.[5] Perhaps Peter was demonstrating that he understood the concept that Christian forgiveness was to be to a much greater level than was their custom, but grossly underestimated how much greater. Others ponder that perhaps Peter wanted to know at what point he would no longer be obliged to forgive a person's repeated offenses. Both of these two speculations miss Peter's point. Jesus responded, "not seven times, but seventy-seven times" (see Matt 18:21-22.) [6] "Seventy-seven" is a hyperbole, meaning we are to forgive over and over,

---

5. W. Robertson Nicoll, *The Expositor's Greek Testament*, vol. 1 (New York, NY: George H. Doran Company, 1917), 241.

6. Some translations have an alternate translation of seventy times seventy (490) rather than seventy-seven times.

not stopping with once or twice, or even dozens of time. According to Jesus, the offer of forgiveness clearly has no quantitative limit.

Forgiveness is a paramount concern—so much so that other important things, such as worship of God and prayer, are to give way to forgiveness and reconciliation: "Therefore, if you are offering your gift at the altar and there remember that your brother or sister has something against you, leave your gift there in front of the altar. First go and be reconciled to that person; then come and offer your gift" (Matt 5:22-23).

The situation that propels us to initiate with our estranged brother or sister is simply that we know that he or she has something against us, legitimate or otherwise. Although some falsely assume that Jesus teaches us to seek reconciliation only if we are willing to admit guilt, we are not exempted from the responsibility to go to the other person just because we have no specific knowledge of what we might have done that caused the strain on the relationship. Nor are we to manufacture a confession and approach our brother or sister with that fabrication in an effort to appease them. Our responsibility is broad. We are to go, guilty or not. We are to be the initiators, just as God first initiated with us. Our effort to process the conflict might be flatly refused by our offended brother or sister. If so, then we are called to entrust the relationship to God and stand ready to rebuild the relationship, if and when the other person indicates that he or she is ready.

Forgiveness Is Merciful

The question then becomes, *how are we to initiate?* Immediately after explaining to Peter that forgiveness of those who hurt us is to be ongoing and without limitation, Jesus tells the story recorded in Matthew 18:21-35, known as the Parable of the Unmerciful Servant. Here, forgiveness is likened to a king who wanted to settle his accounts with his servants who owed him money. The first servant to be dealt with was in default. He owed the king ten thousand talents, equivalent to approximately $4.8 million US—a sum impossible for an ordinary man to repay. The servant was sentenced to be sold, along with his wife, his children, and all their possessions so that the proceeds could be used to repay the debt. The servant fell on his knees, begged for patience, and promised that he would pay it all back. The king took pity on him and forgave his entire debt, setting him and his family free. Later, when the forgiven servant discovered that a fellow servant owed him the equivalent of $8 US, he began to choke him demanding that he pay the $8 debt. The man fell on his knees, begged for patience, and promised to pay him back. But the servant who had been forgiven by the king refused to grant an extension and had his fellow servant thrown into prison. When the other servants reported to the king what had happened, he summoned the servant whose enormous debt had been forgiven and called him wicked. The king said, "I canceled all that debt of yours because you begged me to. Shouldn't you have had mercy on your fellow servant just as I had on you?" (Matt 18: 32-33). The king angrily turned this servant over to the jailers to be tortured, until he should pay back his entire debt. Jesus concludes this story with the warning, "This is how my heavenly Father will treat each of you unless you forgive a brother or sister from your heart" (Matt 18: 35).

If we are unwilling to forgive those who have caused us hurt, our heavenly Father will not forgive us. There is a direct connection between our individual reconciliation with God, and whether we are merciful to those who have wronged us. Over and over Jesus affirmed the theme of mercy. The Lord's Prayer found in Matthew 6:12 (NLT) states, "Forgive us our sins, as we have forgiven those who sin against us." Gerald Borchert writes, "Many Christians fail to recognize that every time we pray the Lord's Prayer we may in fact be calling on God to send judgment and condemnation upon us.… Jesus gave us a warning of the way we are to live. Failure to recognize this warning can be devastating in its consequences."[7] The warning implicitly calls

---

7. Gerald L. Borchert, Ph.D, *Assurance and Warning* (Singapore: Word N Works, 2006), 343.

and encourages us to share in God's heart. This prayer makes it clear that as we ask for forgiveness of our sins, we have already forgiven those who have sinned against us. As we seek mercy for ourselves, we are extending mercy to those around us.

Use of this model prayer is the custom in many Christian communities today. It was a prayer that was to be prayed together—not just alone. If praying this together is not a part of your Christian tradition, perhaps you might consider Jesus' encouragement to pray this way privately. When we pray this together, we are privileged to participate in the nature and heart of God which is the core of worship. Thus, anytime we truly offer forgiveness to those who hurt us we are worshiping God. Furthermore, as his forgiving nature is strengthened within us, our spiritual formation is deepened.

Forgiveness Does Not Retaliate

Our goal is a rebuilt relationship and our method is a unilateral, open-minded extension of forgiveness motivated by *agape* love and imbued with the same quality of mercy that God has extended to us. It follows, then, that we must not return evil in any form, even when our brother or sister continues to harbor judgments against us for injuries real, imagined, or simply arising from a terrible misunderstanding. We must always leave the way open for reconciliation. The apostle Peter stated, "To this you were called, because Christ suffered for you, leaving you an example that you should follow in his steps. He committed no sin, and no deceit was found in his mouth. When they hurled their insults at him, he did not retaliate; when he suffered, he made no threats. Instead, he entrusted himself to him who judges justly" (1 Pet 2:21-23). No matter the level of suffering that we experience at the hands of others, we are never to attempt to punish them for their actions. Paul addressed this subject in his letter to the Romans where he wrote,

> Do not repay anyone evil for evil. Be careful to do what
> is right in the eyes of everybody. If it is possible, as

far as it depends on you, live at peace with everyone. Do not take revenge, my friends, but leave room for God's wrath, for it is written: "It is mine to avenge; I will repay," says the Lord. On the contrary: "If your enemy is hungry, feed him; if he is thirsty, give him something to drink. In doing this, you will heap burning coals on his head." Do not be overcome by evil, but overcome evil with good. (Rom 12:17-21)

In Paul's letter to the Thessalonians, he addresses the recipients as brothers and sisters, clearly writing to Christians. He charges them, "Make sure that nobody pays back wrong for wrong, but always strive to do what is good for each other and for everyone" (1 Thess 5:15). Christians are not to retaliate against anyone, whether that one is a Christian or not. Should the other person take no responsibility or show no sign of repentance, we are never free to retaliate. In forgiveness we give up our right to get even. When we are tempted to retaliate, we should, instead, see it as an opportunity to forgive and respond in love and thus exhibit the heart of God to those who hurt us.

Forgiveness Can Lead Us to Intervention

Although we are never to retaliate against those who have sinned against us, Jesus' and Paul's injunctions against returning evil for evil do not rule out the possibility of intervention to preclude the ongoing destruction wreaked by the offender on us or others. The Scriptures are replete with examples of intervention with the aim of forgiveness and reconciliation.

One of the most dramatic interventions in Scripture is recorded in John's gospel. Hoping to goad Jesus into making a statement that they could use as a basis of an accusation, the Jewish religious leaders brought to him a woman who had been living in adultery.[8] She had been caught in the act, and we have no scriptural

---

8. See John 8:1-11.

testimony that she had yet repented from her ways. They quoted Moses' command to stone adulterers, then, before the crowd of onlookers, put Jesus on the spot, asking, "Now, what do you say?" In response, Jesus stooped to the ground and wrote in the dirt with his finger. (Although Scripture does not identify what he wrote on the ground, I have always suspected that he listed the sins of her accusers or, perhaps, the names of the women with whom they had committed adultery. But this is complete speculation on my part.) When they persisted in asking him, Jesus finally replied with a single stunning statement: "Let any one of you who is without sin be the first to throw a stone at her." Conscious-stricken, one by one, they left and Jesus then said he would not condemn her and that she should go and no longer live that way.

Scripture provides numerous examples of those among God's people who were called to intervene in the lives of others. Among the most well-known is the Old Testament prophet, Nathan, who intervened in the lifestyle of King David, confronting the King after he had murdered a man in order to take his wife for himself.[9]

To the church at Galatia, Paul gave instruction about intervention: "Brothers and sisters, if someone is caught in a sin, you who live by the Spirit should restore that person gently. But watch yourselves, or you also may be tempted" (Gal 6:1). Jesus gave reluctant consent for divorce under certain situations, which can be understood as a type of intervention.[10]

God calls us to speak the truth in love to those within the Christian community.[11] The author of Proverbs wrote, "As iron sharpens iron, so one person sharpens another" (Prov 27:17). He also wrote "Better is open rebuke than hidden love. Wounds of a friend can be trusted, but an enemy multiplies kisses" (Prov 27:5-6). It was in keeping with these Scriptures that Jesus intervened to cleanse the

---

9. See 2 Sam 12.
10. See Matt 5:31-32.
11. See Eph 4:15.

Temple. Outraged by the presence of the money changers, he drove the merchants from the Temple.[12]

Intentional intervention is not limited only to those who are doing harm. It can extend to people victimized by wrong doing or by unforeseen circumstances not brought on by the victim. In Jesus' parable of the Good Samaritan, a man intervened to help a man wounded by robbers.[13] The most astonishing dimension of the story was not that this man whose religious beliefs were questionable to the Jews was the only one to mercifully intervene. Instead, it was that the 'good, religious leaders' did not. The parable was a thinly veiled rebuke of those who, in the community of faith, have both the responsibility and the power to intervene, but are not sufficiently moved by another's suffering to take action. The actions of these religious leaders form a stark contrast with those of the paralytic's friends, who, in the familiar gospel story, took the initiative to bring him to Jesus for healing.[14] Because there was such a crowd at the home where Jesus was teaching, they made an access hole in the roof, and then lowered their friend through the ceiling, right in front of Jesus. Jesus addressed the ones who intervened on the lame man's behalf, saying that as a result of *their* faith expressed in action, the paralytic was not only healed, but his sins were forgiven as well. Note, it was not the faith of the lame man, but the faith and actions of those who interceded on his behalf, which Jesus affirmed.

When someone helps another become conscious of a problem area to which the latter is blind, God is helping that person grow. In certain situations rebuke is an intervention needed. As we have seen earlier, "Better is open rebuke than hidden love" (Prov 27:5). Luke advises us that "If a brother or sister sins against you, rebuke them; and if they repent, forgive them" (Luke 15:3). Lest we be too anxious to take on this mission of rebuking those who hurt us, we must carefully discern what this Scripture does and does not state. Some

---

12. See Matt 21:12-13.
13. See Luke 10:30-37.
14. See Matt 9:1-2, Mark 2:1-12, and Luke 5:17-20.

might understand it to mean, "If a brother offends you, rebuke him. If he does *not* [emphasis added] repent, then do not offer forgiveness." Interpreted this way, the statement becomes a great 'excuse' to continue the bitterness and hatred of the one inflicting pain upon us, withholding love because there has been no offer of repentance. This contradicts volumes of Scripture. We do not repent to *earn* God's forgiveness. Enemies do not repent in order to earn *our* forgiveness. Jesus extends a heart of forgiveness "while we are still sinners."[15] We are not reconciled without repentance, but God offers us forgiveness, which we can accept as a gift. When we follow through with our confession and repentance, then we are reconciled. God's offer of forgiveness is also our example to follow in our conflicted relationships with one another. If we hold back our forgiveness, awaiting a confession, we are blocking God's divine steps of reconciliation for which he holds us accountable.

Although we might be called to rebuke someone, the writer of Proverbs established that there is no universal mandate to rebuke others. "A wise child heeds a parent's instruction, but a mocker [a scoffer or one who ridicules] does not respond to rebukes" (Prov 13:1). Yet, when we do rebuke or admonish someone, our agenda must be that of love and helping them to see what they do not see about their heart and behavior. There should be no sense of scolding or shaming on our part, but rather an encouragement for them to love and live as Christ lived with us.

When we decide to intervene by exhortation or rebuke, we are presented a great temptation to become a perpetrator of spiritual abuse. Tragically, certain individuals believe they are responsible to God to compel others to improve their moral behavior or correct their theological perspective. Christian leaders seem especially prone to this temptation. However, each one of us is accountable to God for all that *we* do. No one is accountable to God for what

---

15. See Romans 5:8.

someone *else* decides to do or not do.[16] Scripture states, "So then, we will all give an account of ourselves to God" (Rom 14:12).

Clearly, while retaliation is never right, intervention for the purpose of bringing mercy and justice is appropriate. Those who intervene must approach such missions with the greatest of humility. Our role with our fellow Christians is to be an encourager, perhaps an exhorter, but never to pronounce judgment against them. When appropriate, judgment is God's responsibility, not ours.

God desires and anticipates the restoration of broken relationships. In Matthew 18:15-17 Jesus provides a healing pattern of intervention for broken relationships within the Christian community. He instructs that when a brother or sister sins against us, we should first go to him or her alone and point out the fault. If the person listens, we will be reconciled. If the person refuses, we are to make a second attempt, taking one or two others with us so that all facts can be established. If the person still does not listen, we are to take the matter before the church. If he or she still refuses to listen, we are to treat that person as we would someone outside the church. While there is discussion about what it means to treat someone as an outsider, the passage warrants no rude, unloving, or otherwise destructive response from the one who has been offended. But it seems appropriate to withdraw from certain levels of trust and intimacy, because the bond of mutual trust and unity of heart has been at least temporarily broken.

This biblical passage is the primary source used by many churches as the basis for formal church discipline. The goal of disciplinary intervention is, presumably, the repentance of those who

---

16. Hebrews 13:17 states, "Have confidence in your leaders and submit to their authority, because they keep watch over you as those who must give an account. Do this so that their work will be a joy, not a burden, for that would be of no benefit to you." This verse teaches that leaders will eventually account to God for the quality of their watchfulness over those they shepherd. The writer does not say that the leaders will be disciplined for the wayward behavior of any Christians who do not follow God. Hence, leaders will be accountable to God should they fail to take responsible, loving initiatives toward those who do not live as God desires.

have sinned and the reconciliation of the fractured relationships. I have seen many examples of its application within local churches, but, sadly, very few instances with the desired outcome. I suspect that there are at least two possible reasons for this. First, it may be that the confronter does not come with a spirit of humility, but, instead, a desire to win. If church leaders approach the task with judgment or arrogance, the one confronted likely will be repelled by their pride and resent any attitude of spiritual superiority. Second, some of the confronted persons are simply so self-willed that they will readily sacrifice relationships within the body of Christ to behave as they wish—no matter what the consequence. When this passage was written, the consequences were dire–the unrepentant person faced the loss of relationships with the entire community. In that day it was difficult to find an alternative Christian community. Today, church discipline is less effective, because it is easy for the offender to simply move on to a different local church. When this happens, however, they take their unrepented sin with them. Ultimately, it will be a barrier to loving relationships elsewhere and lead to isolation that, while not physical, is no less profound.

Although an intervention might fail and reconciliation can remain elusive, our offer of forgiveness is, nevertheless, still possible and in fact, necessary if we wish to avoid the same fate as the unrepentant person.

Forgiveness Is Not Boastful

In Scripture we often are exhorted to forgive all those who offend us, but nowhere are we exhorted to *tell them* that we forgive them. There are times that telling someone that we have forgiven them demonstrates mercy and is an affirmation of our love for them, particularly if they have directly asked for our forgiveness. But announcing the news of our forgiveness is problematic when the recipient has not sought our forgiveness. The apostle Paul writes, "Love is patient, love is kind. It does not envy, it does not boast, it is not proud" (1 Cor 13:4). Our pronouncement of forgiveness could reveal pride on our part. This destructive character quality is sure to drive others away—especially those who are living apart from God.

Furthermore, we cannot assume that those we are ready to forgive are ready to accept our forgiveness. Defensive barriers might still exist, perhaps because we have not earned the other's trust yet. From the other's point of view, this declaration of forgiveness merely articulates a negative judgment that we hold against that person. If our assessment about the other's actions is just and we have forgiven him or her, we need not proclaim our forgiveness. Conversely, if our assessments were unjust or have no basis in fact, a magnanimous declaration of forgiveness can introduce yet another barrier to an already blocked relationship, for which *we* now must be forgiven.

Our forgiveness, whether explicitly disclosed or not, should not to be calculated to manipulate our desired resolution or to make us 'look good'. Paul warned the Philippians "Do nothing out of selfish ambition or vain conceit" (Phil 2:3a). Instead, our forgiveness is to be offered to others before God as a reflection of, and a fitting response to, God's forgiveness, which we enjoy day after day. That offer of forgiveness, then, can be used by the Holy Spirit as he sees fit.

Forgiveness Provides Unity

The Didache is generally attributed to the ancient church leaders late in the first century and arguably one of the earliest surviving documents from the ancient church. It was a widely used instruction manual for church practice during the germinal period of the church. Although it does not have the authority of Scripture, it boldly and clearly summarizes the scriptural imperatives we have discussed about how to live in loving and mutually respectful relationships with one another. *The Didache* 1:2-4 states,

> The way of life is this: "First, thou shalt love the
> God who has created you; second, your neighbor
> as yourself. Whatever you do not want to happen
> to you, do not do to another." This is the teaching

[that comes] from these words: Bless those who
curse you, and pray for your enemies, and fast for
those that persecute you. For what grace do you
expect if you (only) love those that love you? Do
not even the nations that? As for you, love those
that hate you, and you will not have any enemy.[17]

This exhortation from *The Didache* is also affirmed in Paul's
words to the Roman Christians, "Bless those who persecute you;
bless and do not curse" (Rom 12:14). Once again we see the theme
of forgiveness and love being extended to one's enemies—clearly
ones who have neither confessed nor repented from their destructive behavior.

The Didache 14:1-2 also echoes the scriptural injunctions to
actively seek forgiveness from those we have offended and to lovingly
intervene to heal broken bonds: "Assembling on every Sunday of the
Lord, break bread and give thanks, confessing your faults before-
hand, so that your sacrifice may be pure. Let none who is engaged
with a dispute with his comrade join you until they have been reconciled, lest your sacrifice be profaned."[18]

This teaching about forgiveness and reconciliation was
taken very seriously within the first Christian communities. In the
ancient church, right relationship with God and others was an absolute prerequisite for participation in the Eucharist (Communion). A
Christian was to voluntarily make every possible attempt at reconciliation before he or she participated again in the Eucharist. The intent
was not to restrict participation in Communion. On the contrary,
this teaching emphasized the centrality of the Eucharist in worship by underscoring the importance of maintaining unity within
the Christian community. This is consistent with Jesus' prayer to the
Father recorded by John,

---

17. Kurt Niederwimmer, *The Didache* (Minneapolis, MN: Fortress
Press, 1998), 64, 73.
18. Ibid., 194.

> My prayer is not for them alone. I pray also for
> those who will believe in me through their mes-
> sage, that all of them may be one, Father, just as you
> are in me and I am in you. May they also be in us so
> that the world may believe that you have sent me.
> I have given them the glory that you gave me, that
> they may be brought to complete unity. Then the
> world will know that you sent me and have loved
> them even as you have loved me. (John 17:20-23)

Unity was to be a joy shared by those within the church and a living witness to the reality of God's love for the benefit of those not yet in the church family. The apostle Paul commended unity to the church in Corinth as God's plan for the body of Christ. "But God has put the body together, giving the greater honor to the parts that lacked it, so that there should be no division in the body, but that its parts should have equal concern for each other. If one part suffers, every part suffers with it; if one part is honored, every part rejoices with it" (1 Cor 12:24b-26). Similarly, to the church in Rome, Paul wrote, "May the God who gives endurance and encouragement give you the same spirit of mind toward each other that Christ Jesus had, so that with one mind and voice you may glorify the God and Father of our Lord Jesus Christ. Accept one another, then, just as Christ accepted you, in order to bring praise to God" (Rom 15:5-7).

This level of unity is impossible without an eagerness to for-give one another in the same manner that God accepted us. To fulfill God's desire for the church, we must embrace the role of a servant and honor especially those who are different from us. He has for-given them just as he has forgiven us. Forgiveness repairs the ties that bind a community in unity. Unity lends the credibility to our words, when we speak to others about the gospel of Jesus Christ.

Chapter 5

Forgiveness Becomes an Act of Worship

As we become more seasoned in our relationship with God, receiving and extending forgiveness will become a natural rhythm in our lives. Forgiveness lies at the heart of God and as we see our relationship with him emerge, we begin to develop a portion of his character in our lives. Consequently, the fundamental question of how we can be in a right relationship with God and have a right connection with one another directly relates to our understanding and practices of worship. Robert Webber spoke directly to the essence of Christian worship when he stated,

> God's vision for the world is remembered and antici-
> pated in worship. Worship is all about how God, [who]
> with his own two hands—the Incarnate Word and the
> Holy Spirit—has rescued the world.... The centerpiece
> of his saving action is the incarnation, death, and res-
> urrection, where sin and death have been defeated and
> where the deliverance of creatures and creation, which
> will be consummated at the end of history, will begin.
> In the meantime, worship is the witness to this vision.[1]

For some people it might seem a bit obtuse to bring up the subject of worship. After all isn't that what people do at church on Sunday morning and in our personal times of private devotion?

---

1. Robert E. Webber, *Ancient-Future Worship: Proclaiming and Enacting God's Narrative* (Grand Rapids, MI: Baker Books, 2008), 66.

Christian theologian David Peterson broadens this myopic under-standing of worship by writing that worship is "ultimately linked with all the major emphases of biblical theology such as creation, sin, covenant, redemption, the people of God and the future hope."[2] Our worship does not begin with our church-like actions, or even our minds, but originates within our hearts. Worship involves all our relationships. Worship is our whole-life response to God with our minds, our will, and our hearts.

Today, the language of the heart is equated with our feelings, but in the ancient church the 'heart' meant one's whole self. Ancient Christians understood the heart to be the seat of all human affec-tions, passions, and intellect.[3] This understanding is made quite clear in the Scriptures by such phrases as "...I will give them singleness of heart and action, so that they will always fear me..." (Jer 32:39) and "For out of the overflow of the heart the mouth speaks" (Matt 12:34b). When our hearts are immersed in the practice of forgiv-ing one another, we are participants in and witnesses to what God is bringing about in his kingdom. We taste what it is like to be in right relationship with one another. One day we will eternally feast on this experience in the reconciled presence of God and all those who have trusted in him. The psalmist addresses how we are now able to be in God's presence. "Who may ascend the hill of the Lord? Who may stand in his holy place? Those who have clean hands and a pure heart" (Psalm 24:3-4a). God requires a pure heart, that is, a life orientation of one's heart and will toward him. Worship, then, is not mere religious activity.

In the Scriptures, the original Greek word which is most com-monly translated 'to worship' is *proskynein*. This word expressed an inward attitude of homage or respect, which the outward gestures of

---

2. David Peterson, *Engaging with God* (Downers Grove, IL: InterVarsity Press, 1992), 17.

3. Montgomery F. Essig, *The Comprehensive Analysis of the Bible* (Nashville, TN: The Southwestern Company, 1951), 232.

bowing or kissing represented.[4] *Proskynein* usually implies humble submission to the will of God or grateful acknowledgment of his initiative. It does not primarily mean supplication.[5] Deuteronomy 10:12-13 exhorts us to serve the Lord our God with all our heart and with our soul and to observe the Lord's commands. This implies that worship is a total lifestyle allegiance to God in all our heart and behavior.[6] The worship of God is not possible for those who indulge in a life of rebellion against God, refusing to forgive one another.[7]

The Hebrew and Greek Scriptures used many different words that are often translated as 'worship'.[8] Those words have a variety of meanings, including service, engaging in religious ceremony, an attitude or outward gestures, representing homage, submission, adoration, reverence and respect. Reverence or 'fear' of the Lord is not just respect; reverence results in faithful obedience. Adoration, a very popular term today when worship is the topic of discussion, is not a form of intimacy with God or an indication of special affection toward him; rather, it is an expression of awe or grateful submission-our recognition of his gracious character and rule[9]. Worship is never the outward physical activities alone; rather it requires inner faith, gratitude, and obedience, which are the prerequisites for acceptable worship. Worship is to be *theocentric,* that is, God centered. He is not to be the object of our worship, but, instead, the subject of our worship.[10] Romans 12:1 exhorts us to present our bodies as living sacrifices of service (worship) to God involving our hearts, minds,

---

4. David Peterson, *Engaging with God* (Downers Grove, IL: InterVarsity Press, 1992), 57.

5. Ibid., p. 85. Also, a supplication is a humble prayer, a request for something.

6. See Josh 22:5.

7. See Josh 24:19-20.

8. David Peterson, *Engaging with God* (Downers Grove, IL: InterVarsity Press, 1992), 55-74, 147-158.

9. Ibid. 73.

10. To learn the significant difference between these two perspectives, examine the presentation by Robert E. Webber in *The Divine Embrace* (Grand Rapids, MI: Baker Books, 2006), 230-239.

and wills through lifestyle of obedience. This lifestyle is characterized by forgiveness, confession, repentance, and reconciliation, which is worship as God understands it.

Scripture indicates that it is only possible to serve the Lord acceptably because of God's gracious initiative in rescuing people from bondage to other masters, and revealing his will to them. The service (worship) of God demands obedience and faithfulness in every sphere of life. Thus, we must not harbor resentment, plot retributions, or cease loving someone because they have hurt us. When we refuse to forgive someone, our action erects a roadblock in our ability to worship God. Our forgiveness of others is the act of worship (humble service) that we must do to exhibit God's love for that person.

Fractured relationships surround most of us in our workplaces, churches, and families. Some people, who see themselves as Christians, are quite indifferent toward ongoing patterns of sin in their lives. Other Christians aren't indifferent, but they harbor grudges, feeling justified in doing so, because they have been deeply hurt by others. When we live this way, our focus is on ourselves, not God. This frame of reference precludes meaningful worship. We worship when we focus on what God has done, is doing, and will do, and then live in light of these truths.

The giving and receiving of forgiveness as an expression of our total allegiance to God is a potent act of worship, and becomes a profound means of our spiritual formation.

Chapter 6

Popular Fictional Myths about Forgiveness

Webster's dictionary defines a myth as "a real or fictional story that appeals to the consciousness of people by embodying its cultural ideals or by giving expression to deep, commonly felt emotions."[1] For clarity, I have added the word 'fictional' to the title of this chapter because the following traditions are not true to the reality of forgiveness. While some of these myths are quite popular, each one of them interferes with effective forgiveness.

Myth 1. In order to forgive someone I must be able to forget what they have done. Forgiving is not connected in any way to forgetting what has happened. Dr. Hamilton Beazley, professor of Philosophy and Religion writes, "With forgiveness, we let go of the past in order to reclaim the present, but we do not forget the past. The memories remain, but their power to hurt us does not."[2] As we forgive others, we can begin to live without being controlled by their bad behavior. We live with the consequences of the wounding, but no longer in angry reaction to it. If we bottle up the real pain we feel and try to ignore the actions of the one who inflicted the pain, we will never reach the point of forgiving the person. Only when we

---

1. *Webster's II New Riverside Dictionary* (New York, NY: The Berkley Publishing Group, 1984), 466.
2. Hamilton Beazley, Ph.D., *No Regrets: A Ten-Step Program for Living in the Present and Leaving the Past Behind* (Hoboken, NJ: John Wiley & Sons, Inc., 2004), 155.

concede the hurt and its consequences can we launch our process of forgiveness.

Myth 2. If I forgive someone, I excuse his or her offensive behavior. Forgiveness does not imply lack of guilt. Rather, it implies the opposite. There is no need to forgive the innocent. If we make excuses for another person's destructive behavior, we are only seeking to erase the pain of the offense. However, rationalizations of destructive behavior do not withstand the passage of time and our pain is guaranteed to return, leaving us in bondage. The only way to freedom is to extend forgiveness. As we forgive someone, his or her offending behavior loses its foothold in our emotions. Then we can begin to move on with our lives.

Myth 3. If I forgive someone, I can no longer hold the person accountable for the offending behavior. God forgives us, but he still holds us accountable. The apostle Paul stated, "So then, we will all give an account of ourselves to God" (Rom 14:12). Likewise, when our actions harm others, or even ourselves, we are also accountable to one another. For example, a divinity student at a prominent seminary submitted a research paper to his professor that exceeded the student's normal performance. As the professor read the paper, it struck him as familiar. The professor went to his library, pulled a volume off the shelf, and discovered that the student had plagiarized several pages. The professor confronted the student and sympathetically listened to the student's contrite statements about how busy he had been and how pertinent the content was to his paper. The professor forgave the student for his plagiarism, and then reported him to the Dean, knowing that severe consequences would follow. As one might expect, the student was immediately expelled. Although the professor forgave, he did not excuse the student's mistake, nor did he fail to hold him accountable.

Each of us might easily find ourselves in a position to hold another person accountable. For example, the state might hope to prosecute a criminal for his actions. Cooperating with the justice system is not inconsistent with forgiving the criminal. It only means that we honestly testify to what we saw and heard. If we attempt to hold someone accountable, we might discover that our efforts are not welcome, even when we join accountability with forgiveness. Although it might tarnish the friendship, accountability is, nevertheless, the appropriate choice. We hope the offender will turn from destructive ways and make restitution. If not, we still forgive. Any vestige of vengeance, retaliation, or bitterness on our part is a clear signal that we have not yet fully forgiven.

Myth 4. I cannot forgive someone that continues in hurtful behavior. Consider the countless examples in Scripture of forgiveness being offered amidst ongoing affliction. Joseph was sold into slavery by his brothers. The negative consequences of that sin lasted for many years. But, he forgave them. Jesus forgave even as he was dying on the cross, despite excruciating physical, spiritual, and emotional pain. When there is an ongoing injustice, we are to forgive even though the offense might continue. Forgiveness is not connected with anyone ceasing their hurtful actions.

We are not called, however, to indiscriminately absorb abuse. Unfortunately, the Bible has sometimes been misused to support this error. For example, when Jesus said, "If someone strikes you on one cheek, turn to him the other also. If someone takes your coat, do not withhold your shirt" (Luke 6:29)[3], he did not expect people to accept mistreatment without protest. Instead, he was instructing his followers to go beyond what the Hebrew and Roman laws allowed. According to Hebrew law, an insulting slap on the face could legally be answered by an equally insulting slap on the face. On the contrary, Jesus' followers are to refrain from "an eye-for-an-eye" justice. Under Roman law, a soldier could order you to give him your outer coat, but the solder was not allowed to take your inner clothing. But Jesus' followers are to give more than what is required. Thus, Jesus' teaching admonishes us to return good for evil, rather than resist evil by doing evil.[4]

---

3. The same teaching of Jesus is also recorded in Matt 5:39.
4. Clifton J. Allen, ed., *The Broadman Bible Commentary*, vol. 8, General

We also should not extrapolate from Jesus' words a prohibition against self-defense or protection of loved ones. As we have seen, certain situations require appropriate intervention, and abuse is certainly one of them.

Myth 5. I can forgive someone, but I cannot possibly have a meaningful relationship with that person. It is true that you may very well never be able to have a restored relationship; there are no guarantees. However, one thing that will forever ensure a permanent break is your unilateral choice to cut the other person out of your life. If you have forgiven the one who hurt you, then you will not be the obstacle in reestablishing a meaningful and respectful relationship with that person. While a fracture might persist because the other person remains unwilling to discuss the matter or take responsibility for his or her own actions, isolation should not be your doing.

However, even if the offender is willing to renew friendly relations, you may never again have the level of security that you need. Rebuilding a broken trust is a long, slow, difficult process that requires a substantial commitment from the offender. Absent that commitment, you may choose to establish a new boundary, different from the level at which you have previously operated, which limits your level of personal disclosure. If the offender is not a safe person and continues his or her destructive behavior or does not recognize your attempts to set new boundaries, then reestablishment of trust will be severely impaired despite your offer of forgiveness. Nevertheless, do not be the one who refuses to attempt reconciliation. If you both reach out and forgive one another and are willing to change and grow, a renewed and meaningful relationship is entirely possible.

Myth 6. Forgiving someone means that I will be fully reconciled with the offender. Hopefully, our desire is always reconciliation, but that assumes both a willingness to reconcile on the other's part and the possibility of contact with the other person.

Articles Matthew-Mark (Nashville, TN: Broadman Press, 1969), 111.

The reestablishment of a broken friendship can be very challenging. There is an old saying, "It is not how much faith you have that makes the difference; it is in whom you place your faith." This is true in our relationship with God, but it is also true in our relationship with one another. When our broken relationship is with someone who is willing to take responsibility for wounds they cause, or one who at least desires to disclose to you the wounding action that he has experienced from you, you are quite fortunate.

When both parties are willing to pursue healing, listening to each other still can be challenging, especially if there is disagreement about the facts. Listening is essential. We must let the other speak her peace without interrupting to offer correction. Each party can learn something from the other's pain. If we count the other person as a gift from God, we can help create a loving environment in which both parties can be open to full redemption.

Sadly, some people, even when given an opportunity to reconcile, never go there. If one person refuses to process a strained relationship in an honest, transparent, meaningful way, then the two of you cannot be reconciled. We see such a situation in the following story. Richard and Jimmy had been good friends for several years. They had traveled together and had many things in common. At one point Jimmy formed a judgment of something that Richard reportedly told a friend about Jimmy. Jimmy was livid, and he called Richard to announce that their friendship was over. He said he never wanted to see or talk to him again. Richard pleaded with him to explain why he was so upset and he wanted to resolve the problem, but Jimmy would not do so. Later, at a social event, Jimmy stood five feet away, looking past Richard as if he were not there. It seemed as though Jimmy was trying to punish Richard; he would not communicate with Richard, directly or indirectly. Other than respectful attempts to initiate a conversation, there was nothing more Richard could do to bring about reconciliation. Richard needs to forgive Jimmy for his intentional isolation and judgments, but they will not return to friendship until Jimmy is willing to open up and process the conflict with Richard.

Myth 7. I cannot forgive someone who doesn't ask me to forgive them. Our sense of fairness is often upset when we purpose to forgive someone who has not yet asked for it. Actually, should a person ask for our forgiveness, we might be tempted to acknowledge their petition graciously, but privately retain our judgment against them. In such a case it is tempting to bypass our most important role in the rebuilding of our relationship—blessing the one who has offended us. It is precisely when a request for forgiveness has not come that we have the greatest opportunity to experience the liberty of forgiveness, because our forgiveness is then entirely unconditional. Accordingly, if the other person seeks us out, the leap toward full reconciliation will be an easy one for us. Meanwhile, an unrestrained and deliberate choice to forgive enables us to enjoy a freedom from bitterness.

Myth 8. If I forgive someone, I am being disloyal to other people that have been hurt by the offending party. Generally our friends think very highly of us, when we forgive someone who hurts us. You might hear the expression, "You are a much better person than I am. I could never forgive them for what they did to you." However, this same person might easily take a very different position when you forgive the offender, if that person has also hurt them or someone close to them! Your wounded friend wants your undivided loyalty and your full support in an alliance against the perpetrator. She will want you to join with her in criticism of the one who caused you both undeserved pain. Any mercy that you extend to the perpetrator might evoke a feeling that you have become disloyal to your friend. This friend feels entitled to limit your forgiveness toward someone else. She might even reject you. There is, sometimes, a false sense of intimacy when two people align themselves against a third. The two might be disinclined to forgive the other because they might lose their sense of intimacy. People with good intentions can fall prey to this thinking because this false intimacy seems like genuine friendship. It is not; nor is this alignment process a part of the historic understanding of forgiveness.

Myth 9. I can only forgive when and if the other person meets my conditions. We might place conditions on our forgiveness even beyond receiving an apology. We may expect restitution for damages done or require that a person suffer separation from us before we will forgive them. When we compile a list of conditions to place on those we need to forgive, we overwrite God's instructions. We open these human-centered agendas in contradiction to God's wisdom. This will not lead to reconciliation. Conditional 'forgiveness' is problematic because down deep it asserts our own righteousness. We deceive ourselves into believing that we have remained faithful to God's desire for reconciliation or that the other person's attitude prohibits us from forgiving them. Conditions only further fracture what is already a painful and hurtful relationship. Forgiveness must be unconditional.

Myth 10. If the other party does not accept my forgiveness, then I have not really forgiven. Just as forgiveness is to be unconditional, its genuineness is not conditional on its acceptance. Forgiveness is our offer, indeed our commitment, to move ahead and no longer impose retribution or demand anything from the other person for their wounding actions. If the other party wants to accept your forgiveness, they will eventually come to believe that they did commit offending acts toward you and feel regret for their actions. Then, hopefully, they will desire to have a renewed relationship with you. Jesus calls us to love our enemies and pray for them.[5] We know that we have forgiven them when they no longer elicit our hostility and we are able to ask God to bless them. Our forgiveness frees us, whether or not the other party accepts our forgiveness.

Myth 11. I have forgiven the person, but when someone mentions his name to me in a conversation, I feel it is important to point out his flaws, because it is the truth. If by saying something negative about

---

5. Matt 5:43-47.

that person, we gain a sense of self-validation, we have succumbed to retribution, which is clear evidence of our unforgiveness. Even if we restrain our overt negative comments, but we still carry covert anger, we are not yet far long on the road to forgiveness. While forgiveness never means forgetting, it does mean that our hostility and retribution cease. Of course we must be discerning and prevent ongoing harm where possible, which might entail sharing negative information with those at risk. Even then, any words that carry with them a sense of retribution or payback are inappropriate and contrary to God's agenda. Although the apostle Paul wrote to the Christians at Ephesus that they were to speak the truth in love[6], being truthful does not mean telling the entire story, especially over and over to person after person! Being truthful does not give us license to publicize other's sins. The level of disclosure in this arena must be guided by God's Holy Spirit, but frankly, I think we should err on the side of not damaging the reputation of others, especially when we are driven to align someone with us against the other person.

Myth 12. Forgiveness is an event, not a process. The process of forgiveness is much deeper than a well-motivated logical choice. It begins with a change in our heart, which must be affirmed again and again. Forgiveness of others is brought into reality by countless ongoing choices we make toward the person who has hurt us. We must break the pattern of withholding love and cancel our tendencies toward retaliation and retribution. This does not happen quickly or easily. As we move into the process of forgiveness, our capacity to forgive is expanded. The initial steps seem to be the most difficult. It is worth remembering that just as our forgiving others is a process, so it is also a process for those who strive to forgive us. We must learn to patiently wait for God to bring about a change of heart in those we have hurt as he helps them become ready to return to a loving relationship with us.

---

6. See Eph 4:15.

Myth 13. Time heals all wounds. Embedded in this statement is one of two self-perpetuating obstacles to reconciliation. If we are the one causing the pain, we probably want to deny our actions and avoid taking responsibility for what we have done. If we are the wounded person, it is likely that we have not been willing to enter the process of forgiveness of the other person. While the passing of time might seem to mitigate pain or guilt, it will never heal any of the wounds. A cut finger can heal over time, but it is not time that affects the healing, rather the intervention that our body does through antibodies and our careful attention to cleanliness and stitches, if necessary. Years after an event has happened we can flash back to that moment of original wounding we received or caused, if we have not received healing. The only length of time that we see in the Scriptures regarding forgiveness is immediate. There is no support for procrastination of reconciliation. Whether we are the one who has been hurt or the one who caused the pain, the intensity of the pain and the urgency of scripture call us to take the initiative to start the process of reconciliation.

Chapter 7
Making Confession

Looking at Confession

Several visual images come to mind when we hear the word 'confession'. None of them are very appealing. One is the image of an apprehended suspect sitting in a police interrogation room. The police ask questions one way and then another, pressuring him to break down and reveal the details of his crimes. They try to intimidate him with falsified evidence. In every way possible they seek to trap him, bombarding him with accusations and offering some special dispensations, should he confess to committing the crimes of which he is accused. They keep at this process continually for hours. When the suspect finally admits his guilt, the detectives rejoice in the completion of their assigned mission. Another image of confession is a small kid who is accused by a much larger boy of some infraction that he did not actually commit. The bruiser exhorts the younger kid to confess, "if he knows what is good for him." Because the younger one is intimidated, afraid for his safety, he recants his innocence and submits to the verdict of guilty as charged. He then suffers humiliation and some form of retribution by the big guy, who needs to demonstrate his prowess to his bruiser friends.

Neither of these images bears any resemblance to Christian-based confession. Confession has no connection with trickery, manipulation, or intimidation. There can be no compulsion by those around us.[1] Furthermore, confession does not mean to admit that you did something, now that your past actions have become undeniably public. Instead, confession for the Christian is a transformational act that begins with an awareness of his or her sin. It is much more than mere acknowledgment of our actions. Confession contains a positive thrust. When we have wounded God or another person, transformational confession opens the door to reconciliation and is ultimately an affirmation.

The word 'confession' has two different but allied meanings. First, it denotes a public stand in support of something. This perspective of confession is a declaration of personal assent and endorsement. An example of this type of confession is when we publicly confess our faith in God. The other meaning is a stand taken against an action that that the confessor now regrets. It is from this perspective that we confess our sins. Of our own free will, we state without reservation precisely what we did. We declare what we believe to be true about ourselves or our convictions, no matter what the consequences. Because confession of sin requires great transparency, it is an intimate act. It involves the heart, not merely the head and requires our full engagement.

An examination of the words of the apostle Paul written to the Christians in Rome reveals much about the ancient understanding of confession. Paul writes, "that if you declare [confess] with your mouth, 'Jesus is Lord,' and believe in your heart that God raised him from the dead, you will be saved. For it is with your heart that you believe and are justified, and it is with your mouth that you profess [confess] your faith and are saved" (Rom 10: 9-10).

These verses are sometimes understood to establish two preconditions for our being made right with God—first, believe, and second, make an oral public announcement of that belief. Some would say the neglect of either one of these distinct actions indicates that we have not met the requirements and, therefore, cannot

---

1. I am not referring to a stricken conscience or the prompting of the Holy Spirit about things that we do that are wrong.

be forgiven. However, this two-fold condition for forgiveness can be traced to an errant Western mindset derived from the English translation of the Scriptures. A look at several key words from the passage in the original Greek will demonstrate how the very different, Middle-Eastern, first-century mindset would have interpreted this crucial statement.

Most significantly, the words 'believe' and 'confess' will show that they are unavoidably interwoven. The Greek word we translate as 'believe' which is used here by Paul is *pisteusēs*. This word includes the Western understanding of believing, but also means to place one's confidence in, to trust. It is much more than mere credence.[2] The scope of the word *pisteusēs* goes well beyond intellectual knowledge. Our confession, says Paul, declares both where we place our confidence and trust and on whom and what we rely.

'Declare' in this verse is the Greek word *homologō*. It is a cognate from *homos*, same, and *legō*, to speak. It means to speak the same thing, to agree with. To confess one's faith would be to agree with God's reality. Likewise, confession of sin is agreeing with God's point of view, or, in the context of human relationships, agreeing with the point of view of the person whom we have hurt. We agree with them about what we have done to them. Both words *pisteusēs* (believe) and *homologō* (confess) imply active engagement, never merely a passive assent to an idea.

The apostle John provides us the assurance of God's forgiveness and more when he writes, "If we confess our sins, he [God] is faithful and just and will forgive us our sins and purify us from all unrighteousness" (1 John 1:9). The Greek word used for confess in this verse is *homologōmen*. It carries the same meaning as *homologō* or 'declare' above. As we have seen, confession can mean to publicly endorse someone or something based upon a deep conviction. Hence, Jesus refers to our acknowledgment of him by using the word

---

2. W. E. Vine, "Believe" in *Vine's Expository Dictionary of Old and New Testament Words,* edited by F. F. Bruce (Old Tappan, NJ: Fleming H. Revell Company, 1981), 116.

that is elsewhere translated 'confess'. He says, "Whoever publicly acknowledges [*homologēsei*] me, I will also acknowledge him before my Father in heaven, But whoever publicly disowns me, I will disown him before my Father in heaven" (Matt 10: 32-33). When the word 'acknowledge' (or confess) is associated with a person's name, it conveys the idea of confessing allegiance to that person. This is precisely what Jesus is stating here. When we have lived a life of declared allegiance to Jesus, he pledges to favorably present us to his Father. Jesus also said that if any do not give allegiance to him, then at the time of judgment, he will give no allegiance to them. Jesus provides both an assurance if we follow him and a warning if we do not. We must listen to both elements of truth.

As we have seen, spirituality is our participation in Jesus' fellowship with the Father. True spirituality means we agree with God's point of view about our actions and take responsibility for them. Only after we acknowledge our sin through confession can we realistically expect God to help us modify our behavior.

According to Richard Leonard, "the Hebrew word for 'making confession' has a nuanced meaning similar to that of its Greek equivalent. It means to confess Yahweh: to 'confess [his] name' (1 Kings 8:33) and to acknowledge his acts on behalf of his people."[3] In the Hebrew worldview, a confession proclaims and acknowledges the historic saving deeds of God. Taken together, these Greek and Hebrew words give confession a strong creedal element. Confession clearly focuses on God and our agreement about what he has done, is doing, and will be doing; it is not primarily about us and what we have done. A lifestyle marked by this type of confession becomes another way that the gospel of Jesus Christ is made known to those outside the community of God.

Transformational confession is an interactive engagement between a person and God, and often others. It is not to be reduced

---

3. Richard C. Leonard, "266-Confession of Sin" in *The Complete Library of Christian Worship*, vol. 1, *The Biblical Foundations of Christian Worship*, Robert E. Webber, ed. (Peabody, MA: Hendrickson Publishers, Inc., 1993), 304.

to psychological liberation or erasure of guilty feelings. Confession of our sins brings healing to us and, hopefully, to others as well. Our confession should also lead us to repentance. Changed behavior always provides a strong catalyst for reconciled relationships, though it does not guarantee reconciliation. Full reconciliation requires *both* persons who are in conflict to participate in the process of forgiveness. Yet, when we are the offender, confession is the beginning point on our journey toward potential reconciliation.

Confession always is directed toward the one who has been offended, either God or another person, and sometimes both. Whether the offense is against God, ourself, or others, genuine confession involves realizing that we have offended another and then acknowledging what we have done. But this acknowledgment has no significance unless we agree with the other person's point of view. The other person may be God or a friend, a family member, a child, or even an enemy.

In all cases we are easily tempted to make excuses for our actions. This is a defensive posture, which must never be confused with confession. When we proffer explanations to provide an excuse for our actions, we are not confessing. We are refuting our guilt, declaring that we are actually innocent. Such ploys will not work with God, nor will they be effective in healing relationships which we have sabotaged by our destructive actions. If, indeed, if we have a legitimate excuse, then we are not guilty and we need no forgiveness. If I drop an expensive work of art because another person carelessly bumps into me, then he, not I, needs to be forgiven.

It can be helpful for us to confess our sins to one another. The apostle James taught, "Therefore, confess your sins to each other and pray for each other so that you may be healed. The prayer of a righteous person is powerful and effective" (Jas 5:16-17). This verse is sometimes narrowly interpreted to mean that we are to confess our sins only to those persons against whom we have sinned. Certainly, our confession often helps the hurt person to start the forgiveness process. But James actually encourages us toward something much broader. A private confession to a safe third party can be a source of support and encouragement as well as challenge. Proverbs 27:17 asserts, "As iron sharpens iron, so one person sharpens another." 'Sharpening' occurs as we confess not only our sins, but also as we confess Jesus to our brothers and sisters in Christ. Only at this level of relationship can we reap the transformational benefit of the practice of biblical confession.

No one ever matures to a point where he or she no longer needs to confess. Throughout the Old and New Testaments we see a repetitive, generational pattern of wrongdoing, confession, repentance, and reconciliation returning to wrongdoing, confession, repentance, and reconciliation followed by more wrongdoing. The cycle does not end. We are born into it, live in it, and once we die, the generations yet to come will keep it going.

Ancient Expressions of Confession

The ancient creeds of the Christian community can be thought of as defining the perimeter of historic Christian beliefs. While these creeds do not give us an expression of the reality of a Christian's experiential relationship with God, and do not carry the authority of Scripture, they do confess the ancient church's fundamental agreement about what God has done and will do. Early in Christian history, divergent theologies (heresies) and practices surfaced which were incongruent with the original understanding of what constitutes authentic Christian faith. Creeds contain a summary of essential Christian beliefs and they were authored both to affirm truth and speak against unorthodox belief. Certain creeds have been recited together in Christian communities for nearly 1,700 years.

Many Christian churches affirm either the Apostles' creed or the Nicene Creed in their worship services every week. Both are ancient, with origins in the second and fourth centuries respectively. Although they are general in nature, they are not ambiguous in their affirmations. Each word was carefully selected, and each had a specific intended meaning. We must be careful not to reduce these statements to a cognitive list of propositions to which one must merely give intellectual assent. Creeds are not merely checklists of Christian orthodoxy; rather, Christians recite them together because they experience the reality of God in their community together. Therefore, when a creed is read aloud, it is never to become some musty incantation that we mumble as we daydream about activities to which we look forward later in the day. Ancient Christian martyrs were not murdered by those who were merely opposed to words written on papyrus; they were slain because those transformational words were written on the hearts of Christians. They held passionate convictions and experienced a fellowship with God that threatened the religious and civil establishments.

Like these early Christians, we should meditate upon these creeds as we consider what they affirm. We can speak them aloud and carefully ponder each of the phases as we confess our faith. When we recall that these confessions have been recited for centuries in many languages and cultures throughout the world, we can feel a part of God's worldwide community.

The first and older of these two is the Apostles' Creed. Many students of theological history believe that it stemmed from the Ancient Roman Creed from the last half of the second century. Much of the content of the Apostles' Creed is virtually identical to that second-century creed. Although it was probably not authored at the hands of the apostles, it is wholly consistent with the teaching and convictions of the original eleven apostles and the churches that they established.

The Apostles' Creed

I believe in one God, the Father almighty,
  the creator of heaven and earth.

I believe in Jesus Christ, his only Son, our Lord:
He was conceived by the the power of the Holy Spirit,
  and born of the Virgin Mary.

He suffered under Pontius Pilate,
    was crucified, died, and was buried.
He descended to the dead.
On the third day he arose again.
He ascended into heaven,
    and is seated at the right hand of the Father.
He will come again to judge the living and the dead.

I believe in the Holy Spirit, the holy catholic[4] Church,
    the communion of saints,
    the forgiveness of sins,
    the resurrection of the body,
    and life everlasting. Amen.[5]

This creed (confession) details that there is only one God (monotheism): the Father, his Son named Jesus, and the Holy Spirit (Trinitarianism). It addresses the major stages of Jesus' life with us: his conception (virgin birth), his birth (the Incarnation), and his suffering, death, physical resurrection and ascension to be with his Father in heaven. This creed affirms that Jesus will physically return to us on earth and judge both those who are still alive and those who have died. It affirms the connectedness of all Christians as a part of the one universal Christian church, the forgiveness of sin, the physical resurrection of our bodies, and the eternal life we share with God and his community. It centers on what he did, is doing, and will be doing. We are in the story, but it is primarily about God (theocentric), not us (anthropocentric).

The Nicene Creed was formulated through the organizational agendas of the Roman emperor, Constantine.[6] In A.D. 325 more than

---

4. Here 'catholic' is not a reference to today's Roman Catholic Church, but the word, instead, means the universal Christian church family into which all believers in Jesus Christ are adopted.

5. *The Book of Common Prayer,* The Apostles' Creed (New York, NY: Seabury Books, Church Publishing Corporation, 1979), 120.

6. Constantine was perhaps converted near the time of his death, so was not known to be a Christian during the time that he removed the death penalty for those who were Christians. He did not make Christianity the formal religion of the Roman Empire. That was done later by Theodosius in 380 A.D.

300 Christian bishops across the Roman Empire traveled to an ecumenical (worldwide) gathering coming from East Africa all the way around the Mediterranean basin to Spain. They met at the city of Nicaea (now Iznik, Turkey). The significant theological issues of that time concerned whether or not Jesus was actually born as God and the larger question of whether or not the Trinitarian understanding of God as Father, Son, and Holy Spirit was accurate. At that gathering Eusebius of Caesarea, the historian, suggested the adoption of an orthodox creed that was used at his church. Because Eusebius' creed did not deal explicitly with the Arian controversy, the creed was not acted upon but enhanced with unambiguous language supporting that Jesus was God from the beginning. It was studied and revised by the 150 bishops who gathered in Constantinople in A.D. 381 and finally read and approved at the Council of Chalcedon in A.D. 451.[7]

The following is the affirmation declared by them and by many Christians to this day. While it provides a more detailed outline of the nature and life of Jesus, it is fully consistent with the earlier Apostles' Creed. These conferences of Christian pastors no doubt labored over the selection of each of these phrases and considered each of them to be important. We would do well to do the same. Once again, I invite you to read this creed aloud and ponder each phrase. Meditate on and confess what it affirms.

The Nicene Creed

I believe in one God the Father Almighty, Maker of heaven and earth, And of all things visible and invisible:

And in one Lord Jesus Christ, the only-begotten Son of God, Begotten of the Father before all worlds, God of God, Light of Light, Very God of Very God,

---

Some historians would argue that Constantine's change to tolerance and later promotion of Christianity was motivated primarily by his desire to unify all of the empire under his command, rather than his personal embrace of Christianity. Constantine was not baptized until shortly before his death.

7. Henry Bettenson and Chris Maunder, ed., *Documents of the Christian Church* (New York, NY: Oxford Press, 1999), 27-29.

Begotten, not made; Being of one substance with the Father, By whom all things were made: Who for us men [men and women], and for our salvation, came down from heaven, And was incarnate by the Holy Ghost [Spirit] of the Virgin Mary, And was made man [human], And was crucified also for us under Pontius Pilate. He suffered and was buried, And the third day he rose again according to the Scriptures, And ascended into heaven, And sitteth on the right hand of the Father. And he shall come again with glory to judge both the quick [living] and the dead: Whose kingdom shall have no end.

And I believe in the Holy Ghost, The Lord and giver of life, who proceedeth from the Father and the Son, Who with the Father and the Son together is worshipped and glorified, Who spake by the Prophets. And we believe one Catholick [catholic] and Apostolick [apostolic] Church. I acknowledge one Baptism for the remission of sins. And I look for the Resurrection of the dead, And the life of the world to come. Amen.[8]

The General Confession

As we have seen, another type of confession is a confession of sin. A widely used confessional prayer is the General Confession. It has been prayed by churches for many centuries. In 1662 the *English Prayer Book* first offered an invitation to all those gathered for public worship to pray the General Confession in unison. Previously, a priest or a layperson prayed on behalf of all those receiving

---

8. Nicene Creed from *The Book of Common Prayer and Administration of the Sacraments and other Rites and Ceremonies of the Church, According to the use of The Church of England* (Cambridge, England: University Press, approx. 1898), 238-239. Contemporary spelling of certain words and two vernacular translated words have been added within brackets by the author. Jesus did not come to redeem only males, but both men and women. Although Jesus was a male, not female, the second use of the word man in this creed is the affirmation of him being human, not just male.

Communion.[9] Although a general confession was never intended to replace our specific prayers of confession to God, this type of public prayer provides a framework upon which we can meditate and add specific details that come to our mind as we express our confessions to God. The General Confession can be the broad contour of our confessional painting offered to God—the specific details you and I add can be the brush strokes and colors that complete the whole.

As you pray through this ancient example of confessional prayer, pause at each phrase and expand each thought with specific details about your life that come to your mind. Include specific sins that you know you have committed and acknowledge the honorable attitudes and actions which are not yet a part of your life. Pray for an obedience that springs from delight in God. Confess to God your allegiance to him.

> Most merciful God, we confess that we have
> sinned against you in thought, word, and deed, by
> what we have done, and by what we have left undone.
> We have not loved you with our whole heart; we have
> not loved our neighbors as ourselves. We are truly
> sorry and we humbly repent. For the sake of your Son
> Jesus Christ, have mercy on us and forgive us; that we
> may delight in your will, and walk in your ways, to the
> Glory of your Name. Amen.[10]

Note the broad, yet specific, scope of this prayer. The confession includes not only our deeds, but our thoughts, words and omissions. It goes beyond mere moralism to our lack of love. It refocuses us on Jesus Christ, but not merely to remember God's acts of the past. In this prayer we also anticipate God's hand upon us in the future and our coming delight in the ways of God. The prayer reveals that external actions alone, however contrite that they appear, do not

---

9. Marion J. Hatchett, *Commentary on the American Prayer Book* (New York, NY: HarperCollins Publishers, 1995), 343.

10. *The Book of Common Prayer* (New York, NY: Church Publishing Corporation, Seabury Press, 1979), 360.

in themselves demonstrate true confession. True confession begins within the heart.

Lamenting Our Sins Reveals Our Confession

Another powerful form of transformational confession is the lament. To lament is to express sorrow, to morn, or to grieve. While the word 'lament' conjures up an image of sackcloth and ashes, self-deprecation, and depression, these images do not convey the biblical meaning of lament. Instead, lament is a means to reframe our anger, sadness, and despair and so draw near to God with a renewed heart for God.

Lament involves a three-step process. First we disclose to God where we are and how we feel. We need no mask of super-spirituality because God is already aware of our most hidden thoughts. We voice to God our sadness, anger, and pain. We complain to God. We don't sugar-coat our situation. We feel the pain of being alone, deserted, betrayed, or being treated unjustly by others. We express our outrage and pain. We speak out our jealousy of those who have the things we so deeply desire. When we do this, we are in the company of all the biblical characters who have shared our experiences and feelings. Like they, we air everything that weighs upon our heart in God's presence. If we cannot find the words we need, we can use the voices in the Scriptures, especially any psalms of lament that particularly reflect our present experience and feelings.

Yet, we do not stop there. We go on to acknowledge the active presence of God in the present moment. We give thanks to God for his many gifts bestowed upon us, not the least of which is his ongoing love. We thank him for his faithfulness through tough times, when everyone else around us seems to fall away.

Finally, we affirm the truth about God to God. We might return to the voices in Scripture that we know to be true, because of God's past work in us in them. We declare (confess) to him who he is and what he has done for us in the past. Our declarations enter our minds and hearts and we are changed in this process. Our affirmations renew our allegiance to God and rebuild our trust in God's present and future work in our lives.

The discipline of lament might be difficult at the onset, but like most areas of spiritual transformation, it becomes easier as we put it into practice.

Summary of the Process of Lament

- Disclose our true feelings to God
  Express complaints, injustice, pain we feel
- Acknowledge the active presence of God in the moment
  Give thanks for his love and faithful provision for us
- Declare to God
  Who he is
  The goodness of what he has done, is doing, and will do

I offer the following study as a scriptural example of the process of lamenting. In Psalm 51 the psalmist laments his own sins, but also approaches God with confidence, upon whose love and mercy he completely relies. Clearly, he confesses Yahweh as he confesses his sins to Yahweh. Slowly read through this psalm of lament and carefully consider the significance of each phrase.

Psalm 51

Have mercy on me, O God,
    according to your unfailing love;
    according to your great compassion
    blot out my transgressions.
Wash away all my iniquity
    and cleanse me from my sin.

For I know my transgressions,
    and my sin is always before me.
Against you, you only, have I sinned
    and done what is evil in your sight;

> so that you are right in your verdict
> and justified when you judge.
>
> Cleanse me with hyssop, and I will be clean;
>   wash me, and I will be whiter than snow.
> Hide your face from my sins
>   and blot out all my iniquity.
>
> Create in me a pure heart, O God,
>   and renew a steadfast spirit within me.
> Do not cast me from your presence
>   or take your Holy Spirit from me.
> Restore to me the joy of your salvation
>   and grant me a willing spirit, to sustain me.
>
> Then I will teach transgressors your ways,
>   and sinners will turn back to you.[11]

The psalmist, in this case, Israel's King David, begins his prayer acknowledging God's faithful, unfailing love, which remains compassionate despite the fact that David has submerged himself in sin. By asking for mercy, he clearly agrees with God's point of view (confession). He bases his fervent plea for forgiveness entirely on God's great loving compassion, not any merit of his own. He goes on to declare his awareness that his actions contradict God's desires. He recognizes that God, rather than he, determines what is right and what is wrong. God is the standard for all human actions[12], including how we run our businesses, treat those we love (or hate), or control our sexual impulses.

David asks God to cleanse him. He draws upon the image of hyssop[13] as the tool for his cleansing. Hyssop was a small bushy plant that, when dried, was well suited for use as a 'brush'. It was used to

---

11. Ps 51:1, 2-4, 7-11, 12-13.

12. W. E. Vine, *Vine's Expository Dictionary of Old and New Testament Words* (Old Tappan, NJ: Fleming H. Revell Company, 1981), 283.

13. Chad Brand, Charles Draber, Archie England, ed., "hyssop" in *The Holman Illustrated Bible Dictionary* (Nashville, TN: Holman Bible Publishers, 2003), 799.

paint the entryways of the Israelite homes with the blood of the Pass-over lambs (see Exod 12:22). The cleansing that David had in mind is not that of scrubbing with soap and water to remove impurities, but a spiritual cleansing much like the deliverance God provided the Israelites at the Passover. It was not something the Israelites were capable of achieving by their own efforts. Likewise, David requests that God would create in him a pure heart and renew a steadfast spirit in him. This petition implies that David's self-will was insufficient; only God's intervention could transform him.

David longs to sense God's presence, manifested by the Holy Spirit, and he seeks a restoration of the joy that was present in his relationship with God prior to the sins that prompted the confession.

He concludes his confession with a promise to teach others who go astray to turn to God so that they, too, can be restored. In this Psalm, David declares that God can affect change and rebuild that which was destroyed and bring forth goodness in David.

This is quite a confession from a man who was coming to grips with his sins of adultery and murder. David had committed adultery with Bathsheba, and then arranged for her husband to be killed in battle. Scripture provides additional background to David's confession. In 2 Samuel 11-12 we learn that the prophet Nathan ingeniously trapped David into condemning his own behavior. As a result David not only confesses his sin to God, but also directly to Nathan, who took the risky initiative to come to David.[14]

Because Nathan courageously spoke the truth to the king, we see in David a model of the appropriate response to our own sin. Our confession is an affirmation of humble submission to God's point of view with respect to all our actions. When we lament as David did, we, too, receive a pure heart from God. We experience renewal, if we begin with our grief but then move on from our own troubled heart to affirm the heart of God and his active presence with us.

---

14. See 2 Sam 12:13.

Our Confession to Those from Whom We Seek Forgiveness

When we realize that by our actions we have hurt another person, we must always go to that person and take responsibility for what we have done. The imperative is the same, whether that person is a valued friend or just an innocent bystander. Taking responsibility means naming the offense to the one we have offended. We are not to wait for someone we have hurt to come to us. Their silence does not imply consent to our egregious actions. People often are reluctant to bring up their hurts with those who have hurt them for a number of reasons. They might be afraid of additional pain at our hands or find us intimidating. Their reticence might be based on misinformation. They might feel partly responsible or consider resolution completely hopeless. Whatever the reason, the other's silence does not exempt us from God's ongoing call to initiate reconciliation. Paul advised the Romans, "If it is possible, as far as it depends on you, live at peace with everyone" (Rom 12:18). Living in peace requires us to ask those we sin against to forgive us.

We must never expect it to be easy to confess our wrong-doings. We will be powerfully tempted to refuse. "Confession might be good for the soul," goes the old saying, but it can be bad for the reputation. But the truth is, acknowledging our offenses is unlikely to cast a dimmer light on our good name than our sinful actions already have. It is the right and appropriate thing to do.

That said, there are times when people confront us with sins that we cannot confess, because we honestly do not see our behavior as destructive. There are two possible reasons: We might, indeed, be faultless or we might have a blind spot.

All of us have blind spots, and this is one reason that we need trusted friends. They can be God's tools for the 'sharpening' that we so desperately need. Truth spoken to us by a trusted friend might be painful to hear, but true friends reveal to us what we cannot see. The writer of Proverbs declares, "Wounds from a friend can be trusted, but an enemy multiplies kisses" (Prov 27:6). If we know a friend wants the best for us, then his or her perception of what has happened in our broken relationship carries much weight. As the proverb suggests, those who only tell us what we want to hear aren't our friends.

However, if these trustworthy counselors are objective and confirm that a blind spot is not the problem and that you are being falsely accused, there is little that you can do to achieve reconciliation. We are not to say we are sorry when we do not believe that we did anything wrong, particularly when we would do exactly the same thing again given the same circumstances. Nevertheless, it is incumbent upon us to exhibit a forgiving attitude—not a superior one. Perhaps further discussion can bring us and our accusers to a common mind.

In the meantime, we can pray that they will receive a heart that desires to restore our broken relationship. We can pray that we will remain merciful and forgiving toward them. In so far as possible, we must not grieve God's heart by blocking reconciliation.

Those who conceal their sins do not prosper, but those who confess and renounce them find mercy.
—Proverbs 27:13

Chapter 8

The Nature of Repentance

Prepare Ye the Way

The word repentance brings to mind an old man wearing a white sandwich-board sign bearing in crudely painted bright red letters the word "Repent!" This prophet parades around the park with little or no connection to any world but his own. He probably does not know those in his audience, nor is he particularly interested in knowing them. His mission is to proclaim our need to turn away from sin. He makes us uncomfortable, and we certainly don't want him to single us out and come over to talk to us. Yet, even when the messenger is less peculiar, we find the message offensive. Who wants to be told that they need to change?

'Repent' is an ancient scriptural admonition. Centuries before Jesus' birth the Old Testament prophet, Isaiah, foretold the coming of a messenger from the wilderness sent from God who would prepare the way for the Lord.[1] This preparer's mission was to call the Jews tenderly to the reality that their hard service had been completed.[2] In the early first century that prophetic messenger was revealed to be John the Baptizer.[3] Matthew 3:2 records that John the Baptizer[4]

---

1. See Isa 40.
2. Isa 40:3 states, "Speak tenderly to Jerusalem, and proclaim to her that her hard service has been completed, and that her sin has been paid for."
3. I call him John the Baptizer rather than John the Baptist, because he was not a Baptist in the sense that we might think of most Baptists today.
4. John the Baptizer was a contemporary of Jesus whose public ministry began a few years prior to that of Jesus in approximately 26 A.D. Known as the

calling the people to "Repent, for the kingdom of God has come near." John's preaching to the Jews emphasized the coming of judgment, as well as the coming of the Messiah. He continued, "Produce fruit in keeping with repentance" (Matt 3:8), calling those that he baptized to live their lives in ongoing repentance and in virtuous living.

Repentance was not some new spiritual formation program that John unveiled in anticipation of Jesus' impending earthly ministry. John was presenting, again, one of God's historic themes. Scripture records that God called his people to repentance through prophets, sages, and poets, from generation to generation. A very short list includes the declarations to Israel by Jeremiah[5], Ezekiel[6], and Amos[7]; Jonah's warning to the citizens of Nineveh[8], the pronouncements of Jesus[9], and the preaching of Mark and Peter[10].

For the most part, the Jews had consistently maintained regular religious rites of repentance. The ten-day-long Festival of Trumpets had been observed for centuries. The festival began with Rosh Hashanah (the start of the new Jewish year) and concluded with Yom Kippur (the Day of Atonement). These holy days were originally observed as penitential and were designed to allow God's people considerable time for reflection on their conduct and God's saving deeds. Although religious rites of repentance were conducted, it does not necessarily follow that authentic repentance was anymore widespread among the Jews than it is today among Christians. Indeed, the nature of religious regulations in first-century Judaism suggests that compliance with regulations was often a poor substitute for true repentance.

Baptizer, he baptized in the desert region of Judea and preached repentance for the forgiveness of sins. See Mark 1:4.

5. See Jer 15:19a.
6. See Amos 4-5 and Ezek 18:30.
7. See Amos 4-5.
8. See Jonah 3:6-10.
9. See Matt 4:17, Mark 1:15, and Mark 6:12.
10. See Acts 2:38; 3:19.

While we do not know for certain how much the Pharisees emphasized repentance, evidence suggests that repentance was not stressed or modeled. The New Testament portrays the Jewish religious teachers among the Pharisees as insisting upon obedience to their many religious rules. For instance, they limited the number of steps that one could take on the Sabbath, attempting to define precisely what violated the practice of Sabbath rest. In their eyes, only those who adhered to the Pharisees' rule had adequately aligned themselves with the moral requirements of God and, therefore, could be considered good Jews. While these leaders taught some worthwhile things, they reduced righteousness to mere compliance. The emphasis on rules bypassed God's desire for a changed heart.[11]

Rulekeeping can be found in many churches today. Conformity to a contrived system of rules appeals to our self-satisfaction and pride and is far less demanding than true repentance. It should concern us whenever religious leaders spurn Christians who do not espouse their system of rules or, even worse, hold in contempt those outside the church who fail to conform to their standards. We must not expect those who do not consciously acknowledge God to live as if they did! Only God perceives the human heart and it is in the heart that all repentance germinates.

On the other end of the spectrum are churches that curtail, or even eliminate, references to sin and repentance. Many churches rightly affirm God's love and belief in Jesus, but fail to oppose sinful living or nurture true repentance. While some believe this makes the gospel more appealing to the masses, such revisionist theology falls short of the good news presented by Jesus. If we are to experience reconciliation within our families, churches, and communities, the importance of repentance must be reclaimed.

---

11. See Jer 31:33, Deut 10:16, and Joel 2:13.

Repentance Is a Verb

Repentance, as it relates to Christian formation, is turning away from one's pattern of sin and destructive behavior and turning toward God. Yet, in its broadest sense, the word 'repent' need not imply that what one ceases doing or thinking is wrong. By way of illustration, let us consider a woman driving her car from New Mexico north to Denver, Colorado, on Interstate 25. She approaches I-70 which will take her either east or west, depending upon which exit she takes at the interchange. Assume that she takes the turn to the east, toward Kansas City across the Great Plains. Now, suppose that after driving for a while, she decides that she would prefer to travel west, instead, and visit Vail, Colorado. To accomplish this she must first make a definite choice in her mind (and will!), then she must exit eastbound Interstate 70, turn around, and reenter the freeway heading the opposite direction. After her turn around we can say that she has repented. For another example, let us turn to a high school football running back, who has just received the ball for the first time in an important game. He begins to run, is nearly tackled but spins out of his opponent's grasp, and then suddenly, he sees a clear path to the goal line! Thrilled, he starts running with all his strength, accompanied by shouts from his teammates, only to realize a few seconds later that they are shouting for him to turn around because he is headed toward his own goal line! Having discerned his error, the running back reverses direction and dashes toward the opponent's goal line. He would have faced grave consequences had he reached the goal line he first pursued. With great passion and commitment, he changed his intention, his direction, and headed toward the correct goal. This player had successfully stemmed off impending disaster by repenting—to the delight of his coach and his fellow students.

In both cases repentance began with a reassessment of the current direction. Minds were changed, new goals were established, and new desires captured their hearts. But repentance was incomplete until they had actively and intentionally modified their behavior and began to move toward those new goals. Repentance, therefore, is not the same as feeling bad about what we have previously done. It might be accompanied by such feelings, but true repentance involves a change of behavior. For the Christian, it involves a shift from behavior that is inappropriate and destructive to behavior that is appropriate and redemptive because we have changed our minds about living contrary to God.[12]

The prolific second-century lawyer and Christian church leader from Rome, Tertullian, (c. A.D. 155-230) stated, "In Greek, the word for repentance is formed—not from the confession of a sin—but from a change of mind."[13] Tertullian explains that repentance does not necessarily imply that one's actions were sinful or otherwise wrong, rather that it indicates a change from a prior purpose. This change can even be the proper response to a change in circumstances. God is said to have repented several times in the Scriptures.[14]

Repentance, therefore, should not be confused with penance. Penance is a punishment or discipline to which we must submit in order to be worthy of receiving forgiveness. We perform actions of penance to bring about a sense of spiritual restoration. Unlike penance, repentance does not begin with an action but originates within the mind and heart. Nonetheless, repentance prompts us to action, even to the point, on occasion, of great personal sacrifice. It drives us to reverse, insofar as this is possible, the consequences of our inappropriate actions against other persons.

---

12. The word frequently used for repentance (*metanoeō*) means to have changed one's mind. See "repentance" as defined by Colin Brown, ed., *New International Dictionary of New Testament Theology*, vol. 5 (Grand Rapids, MI: Zondervan), 357.

13. Tertullian, *A Dictionary of Early Christian Beliefs* (Peabody, MA: Hendrickson Publishers, Inc.), 174. (c. 207, Ante-Nicene Fathers, vol. 3, 316.)

14. In I Sam 15 God repents from having made Saul king after Saul disobeys Samuel. In Jer 18 God promised to change his mind regarding punishment when a nation turns to obedience. Repentance is a change in intent that issues forth in actions, not just a change in one's intellectual understanding on a matter.

We must not assume that if we are the one who has been hurt by someone else's wrongdoing that we have no obligation to repent. Those who are hurt are often tempted to retaliate or withhold forgiveness from the perpetrator. God entreats us to confess and repent from this behavior even as it germinates in our heart.

The interior change we experience as we repent results in even deeper Christian formation.

Repentance is Our Calling

Unlike other letters to churches where Paul specifically addressed problems in their churches, his letter to the Christians in Rome presented a sweeping introduction and overview of the Christian gospel. Paul saw that both the Gentile and Jewish cultures failed to understand God's way of reconciling the world to himself and that *all* people needed to repent. Early in the letter (Rom 1:18-32) Paul spoke with the perspective of the Gentile in mind. He boldly explained why Gentiles needed to repent. Paul then looked at the prevailing Jewish point of view (Rom 2:1-3:8), showing why the Jews, also, needed to repent.[15] He observed that the Gentile basis for righteousness was primarily behavioral. Yet, they were living lives that were shameful. He then rebuked those who were presuming some entitlement based on their Jewish lineage and their education on the law. Finally, he concluded with a summary and thunderous exhortation that *all* persons need to repent when he wrote, "for all have sinned and fall short of the glory of God" (Rom 3:23). This three-tiered approach was necessary because both Jews and Gentiles were tempted to see themselves as favored by God for reasons that were not the basis or process for reconciliation as revealed by God through Jesus.

In chapter one Paul confronted them about their blind hypocrisy. They had passed judgment against others for doing what

---

15. Gerald L. Borchert, *Worship in the New Testament* (St. Louis, MO: Chalice Press, 2008), 86-89.

they themselves were doing. Paul declared, "Now we know that God's judgment against those who do such things is based on truth. So when you, a mere human, pass judgment on them and yet do the same things, do you think you will escape God's judgment? Or do you show contempt for the riches of his kindness, tolerance and patience, not realizing that God's kindness is intended to lead you to repentance?" (Rom 2:2-4). God's judgment is always based on the facts. Any attempt on our part to re-script or reframe those facts to make them appear otherwise is futile. None of us hold any privileged exemptions from God's just assessment.

As we have seen, many first-century Jews believed that the privilege of their birth as Israelites, alone, would ensure their entrance into the kingdom. This notion of special privilege from God also had seeped into the church in Rome. The Roman Christians felt free to condemn in others what they tolerated in themselves. Paul points out that receiving forbearance and kindness from God should have made them more quickly inclined toward repentance.[16] Paul makes it clear that, "God will repay everyone according to what he has done" (Rom 2:6). This applies even to Christians. A true spirit of repentance will lead us to examine ourselves for those shortcomings we so easily condemn in others. When we begin to see how we live the same way as those we accuse, we also begin to experience the transforming love of God, drawing us toward repentance.

Christian repentance always involves a turn away from sin as we turn toward God. Many times, it is not *only* a turning toward God, but it also involves a humble, contrite turn toward those persons whom we have offended. Whether the wounds were intentional or unintentional, we are to approach those we have wounded in the same way that we are to approach God. When we admit what we have done and ask for the other's forgiveness, it is a sign of genuine repentance. It provides the other person an opportunity to return to us with reduced fear of ongoing injury.

---

16. W. Robertson Nicoll, *The Expositor's Greek Testament* (New York, NY: George H. Doran Company), 595.

As repentance becomes an ongoing part of our Christian life, there will be times when we have the opportunity to assist others as they discover their need for ongoing repentance. This type of help, of course, is completely counter-cultural in most of our communities today. To an extent, this is understandable, because some Christians, like the Roman Christians Paul rebuked in Romans 2, seem to thrive on pointing out other people's shortcomings, while they remain oblivious to their own. Nonetheless, in the Scriptures we see several positive examples of Christians exhorting other Christians within the church to repent. Lest we be too zealous about taking on such a cause, we must consider the following advice from Jesus. As is often the case with Jesus' wisdom and assurances, there are warnings that must be heeded. Matthew records this challenge:

> Do not judge, or you too will be judged. For in the same way you judge others, you will be judged, and with the measure you use, it will be measured to you. Why do you look at the speck of sawdust in someone else's eye and pay no attention to the plank in your own eye? How can you say, "let me take the speck out of your eye," when all the time there is a plank in your own eye? You hypocrite, first take the plank out of your own eye, and then you will see clearly to remove the speck from the other person's eye. (Matt 7:1-6)

Jesus warns us that we will be judged by the same standard we apply to others. While this does not preclude pointing out other's shortcomings, the prerequisite is that we first see our own sins clearly. This is possible only through our own ongoing process of confession and purification through repentance. Only then can we graciously bring revelation and correction to a brother or sister. Our boldness must be undergirded with the meekness to receive encouraging correction from others. What someone shares with us might be from the heart of God and, therefore, we must be anxious to hear their assessments and then take them to God and seek either conviction or release from what we have heard. As Paul wrote to the Galatian

Christians, "Brothers and sisters, if someone is caught in a sin, you who live by the Spirit should restore that person gently. But watch yourselves, or you also may be tempted. Carry each other's burdens, and in this way you will fulfill the law of Christ" (Gal 6:1-2).

The image of carrying each other's burdens can be understood in two ways. In the most popular image, we are to come alongside our sister or brother and share in their experience of pain because of the injustices put upon them. We validate their feelings. While this would be admirable behavior, to act in sympathy is not the teaching of this passage. Instead, Paul is saying that when fellow believers do not see their destructive behavior and, therefore, cannot live in the just and loving way of God, we must come alongside and put our shoulder to the task. We are to disclose lovingly and humbly that to which they are blind. Our call is never to compel the friend to live differently, it is rather to help them, if possible, to see the error of their ways.

Matthew records the challenging words of Jesus, "If a brother or sister sins against you, go and point out the fault, just between the two of you. If they listen to you, you have won them over" (Matt 18:15). The exhorter is cautioned to do this with great humility because there is a great risk for further destruction to the relationship should you already be in a crisis. If there is any sense in which we who confront indicate that we are better or more pleasing to God than the other person, then the confrontation will be rendered not only ineffectual but destructive as well.

The messenger that presents a 'fault' to the hearer is not judge and jury and has no responsibility or right to demand conformity to their point of view. Paul makes clear that each one of us is solely responsible to God for our actions when he writes, "So then, we will all give an account of ourselves to God" (Rom 14.12). Messengers are to be God's agents who speak so that God's Holy Spirit can convict people's hearts. They hope their message will lead to repentance, but they leave the outcome to God. Although the consequences for the unrepentant are also clear—either temporal or eternal separation from God and continued conflict in relationships with one another[17]—only God judges rightly enough to impose those consequences.

It is good to remember that while we may want to urge our friends to repent, it is ultimately God who inspires people to change. The power to repent comes from him. Still, there are appropriate ways to encourage one another to repent. In Paul's first letter to Timothy, the apostle tells Timothy to be gentle with those who oppose his teaching about Christian living. He writes, "Opponents must be gently instructed, in the hope that God will grant to them repentance leading them to a knowledge of the truth, and that they will come to their senses and escape from the trap of the devil, who has taken them captive to do his will" (2 Tim 2:25-26). Paul anticipates that Timothy's gentle teaching and encouragement will help those who are being deluded by Satan to repent. Clear, understandable teaching, delivered in love, can be used by God as a seed in the other person that grows into repentance. It is important that the content of our teaching and encouragement be sound, and the presentation gentle—an exemplary demonstration of God's grace. The teacher/encourager must not use compulsion. If we attempt to make people feel shame or employ other methods of manipulation to bring someone to 'repent', our actions will work against the fruit God is laboring to inspire in them.

This does not mean we are to be timid! Gentleness is not timidity. Paul also told Timothy, "For the Spirit of God not does not make us timid, but gives us power, love, and self-discipline" (2 Tim 1:7). We must be bold, but not obnoxious, since in that case our method will become our message on this matter. Our effectiveness is not ultimately based on the words we use. We must remember that it is the role of the Holy Spirit to convince others of their need to repent. Jesus taught his disciples, "Unless I go away, the Advocate [Holy Spirit] will not come to you; but if I go, I will send him to you. When he comes, he will prove the world to be in the wrong about sin

---

17. Rom 6:23, Rev 21:18.

and righteousness and judgment; about sin, because people do not believe me; about righteousness because I am going to the Father, where you can see me no longer; and about judgment, because the prince of this world now stands condemned" (John 16:7-11). We may be called to be the messenger to share what we see, but God has sent the Holy Spirit to be his Advocate. God desires to use each of us as a gracious facilitator, drawing one another to repentance. This process of drawing others to repentance is clearly a gift from God, for which we may be thankful.

> *Hark, the Herald's voice is crying*
> *In the desert far and near,*
> *Bidding all men to repentance*
> *Since the Kingdom now is here.*[18]

Repentance Is Internal and External

As we have seen, God has persistently called his people to repent of their sins. One such instance occurred after the first temple was dedicated in Jerusalem somewhat before 900 B.C. During a time of adversity, the Lord appeared to Solomon and told him, "If my people, who are called by my name, will humble themselves and pray and seek my face and turn from their wicked ways, then I will hear from heaven and will forgive their sin and will heal their land" (2 Chr 7:14). This message was directed to God's people, not the unbelieving Gentiles. From its foundation, the nation of Israel was to be a model. The outward lives of its people were to reflect internal realities: They were to know and honor God in their hearts.[19] They were to practice humility and put off arrogance. This was to result in a lifestyle of walking with God. However, the Israelites failed to walk with him. God then told them that if they turned away from their

---

18. From the hymn, *Comfort, Comfort, Ye My People by Johann Olearius* (1611-1684 A.D.) and taken from Isa 40:1-5.
19. See Deut 4:29, 6:5.

evil ways and turned toward God, then he would forgive their sins. Healing would come to their community as people lived in right relationships with God and one another.

Several generations later, God delivered a similar message through the prophet Isaiah. God was sickened by Israel's unjust and rebellious deeds and counterfeit worship. His people had focused on scheduled worship programs and structured activities while neglecting a repentant and virtuous lifestyle. Isaiah proclaimed that even religious-looking prayers with arms extended to God are to no avail, because his people have not lived out of a transformed heart that follows God. The prophet Isaiah wrote:

> Your New Moon feasts and your appointed festivals I hate with all my being. They have become a burden to me; I am weary of bearing them. When you spread out your hands in prayer, I will hide my eyes from you; I will not listen. Your hands are full of blood; wash and make yourselves clean. Take your evil deeds out of my sight! Stop doing wrong, learn to do right. Seek justice, encourage the oppressed. Defend the cause of the fatherless, plead the case of the widow. "Come now, let us reason together," says the Lord. "Though your sins are like scarlet, they shall be as white as snow; though they are red as crimson, they shall be like wool. If you are willing to be obedient, you will eat the best from the land; but if you resist and rebel, you will be devoured by the sword." For the mouth of the Lord has spoken. (Isa 1:14-20)

With these words, Isaiah warned the people to repent and live a life of obedience. Should they reject God and fail to turn to him, God warned that they would be devastated. The prophet reiterated God's eagerness to forgive, saying, "Seek the Lord while he may be found; call on him while he is near; Let the wicked forsake their ways and the unrighteous their thoughts. Let him turn to the Lord and he will have mercy on them, and to our God, for he will freely pardon" (Isa 55:6-7). The Israelites were told repeatedly to turn away from their self-centered and sinful behavior and turn toward God. Both their inner thoughts and their outer ways were to change. Biblical repentance has always stipulated both a changed heart and changed behavior. About 150 years after Isaiah, the prophet Ezekiel called Israel once again to repentance when he proclaimed,

> Therefore, house of Israel, I will judge each of you according to your own ways, declares the Sovereign Lord. Repent! Turn from all your offenses; then sin will not be your downfall. Rid yourselves of all the offense you have committed, and get a new heart and a new spirit. Why will you die, house of Israel? For I take no pleasure in the death of anyone, declares the Sovereign Lord. Repent and live! (Ezek 18:30-32)

In this, as in all these ancient Scriptures, God beckoned his people to change their hearts and turn toward him. This would in turn change their behavior. As we have seen, repentance begins in our heart and then our changed heart empowers us to turn toward God and toward one another. The restructuring of our outward actions happens not simply through our fortitude and self-discipline, but as a natural consequence of living in the light of our confessions: change begins to emanate from our hearts. Any attempt to exert our willpower to modify our behavior without embracing God's point of view from our heart will ultimately be futile, even if we appear to be successful in the short-term. Such willful retrenchment in ostensible righteousness can never rival the capacity that God can give us to walk in humility and in love. True repentance involves 'seeing' differently from a radically different perspective, the perspective of our Heavenly Father. It is the 'mind of Christ'. This shift is at the core of our transformational process and comes from God. Consequently, repentance becomes cyclical in nature. Inner shifts in our hearts produce external changes that allow for increasing internal changes, and so on. We no longer retaliate when we are hurt. In so far as possible, we make restitution to those who have received harm or endured hardship as a result of our actions or inaction. This change in our hearts has far-reaching consequences.

The inseparable connection between a repentant heart and repentant actions is quite consistent with the interconnection between faith and works, which is addressed by James, a pillar of the early church. "What good is it, my brothers and sisters, if people claim to have faith but have no deeds? Can such a faith save them? …But someone will say, 'You have faith; I have deeds.' Show me your faith without deeds, and I will show you my faith by what I do. You believe that there is one God. Good! Even the demons believe that— and shudder" (Jas 2:14, 18-19). Confession without repentance is like faith without works. In both cases the former is inseparable from the latter.

Right living (orthopraxy) is never to be in opposition to right belief (orthodoxy). Correct belief will help transform our lives into right behavior. Right behavior must be rooted in right belief. Christian repentance is not simple assent to orthodox theology or belief; repentance comes about through a changed heart with God at the center. Fitz Allison, retired Episcopal Bishop of South Carolina speaking of wrong belief stated, "Heresy is largely a 'matter of the will' and orthodoxy is not correct logic but a mending of the heart."[20] Righteous living always starts with a heart that is turned toward God. Repentance means standing before God and submitting to his verdict of guilty.[21] Living a life of repentance with those whom we hurt is no different from the process we live out with God. We confess (right behavior) to those whom we hurt that we are guilty (right belief) for their wounds. This distinguishes us from most of society. Our confession to those whom we have hurt creates space for the process of reconciliation to begin. Thorough repentance of sins is a

---

20. C. Fitzsimons Allison, *The Cruelty of Heresy: An Affirmation of Christian Orthodoxy* (Harrisburg, PA: Morehouse Publishing, 1994), 35.
21. James B. Torrance, *Worship, Community & The Triune God of Grace* (Downers Grove, IL: Intervarsity, 1996), 78.

prerequisite for thorough reconciliation with all of those with whom we live.

It is not only harmful actions that call for repentance. Destructive thoughts, even those we do not act upon, might also give rise to the need for repentance. Some would argue that having thoughts on which we do not ultimately act cannot be sinful. Such a perspective denies what we see in Scripture. Simon the Sorcerer offered money to Peter to buy the power of the Holy Spirit. Peter exhorted Simon to repent of his desire to purchase the ability to dispense the Holy Spirit.[22] Jesus warned that the sin of adultery already has been committed in a man's heart when he looks at a woman lustfully.[23] Certainly acting on destructive desires brings forth more dire consequences than simply pondering the ideas, but it is in the initial thought that we turn away God. Given that the essence of sin is to turn away from God, it should be clear, then, that we are to repent (turn from sin and toward God) in both our thoughts and deeds. The call to repentance asks for absolute surrender to God in every area of our life, including our thoughts, agendas, and actions toward everyone within our circle of influence. There can be no private, guarded arenas where we claim autonomy from God.

Repentance cannot be solely an internal experience. Repentance is never a private matter limited to a change of mind. Neither can repentance be only a change in our public behavior. Inner repentance is of no value unless it produces a 'Godward' life culminating in changed behavior. The inner and outer dimensions cannot be separated if our repentance is to be biblical repentance.

Repentance Is Non-negotiable

We have seen that God's call to repentance resounded throughout the Old Testament. The New Testament reaffirms the Old Testament's emphasis on repentance. After Jesus' time in the

---

22. See Acts 8:18-23.
23. See Matt 5:27-28.

wilderness, he began to preach, "Repent, for the kingdom of heaven has come near" (Matt 4:17b). Jesus also sent out his disciples to preach that people should repent.[24] Jesus addressed some in Jerusalem, who assumed that people who experienced great disasters were more sinful than others who were more fortunate, when he exclaimed, "I tell you, no! But unless you repent, you too will perish" (Luke 13:5). Jesus insisted that everyone must repent. At one point his disciples were arguing among themselves about which of them was the greatest in the kingdom of God. Jesus confronted their competitive ambitions with, "Truly, I tell you, unless you change and become like little children, you will never enter the kingdom of heaven. Therefore, whoever takes a humble place—becoming like this child—is the greatest in the kingdom of heaven. And whoever welcomes one such child in my name welcomes me" (Matt 18:3-5).[25] In this new way, Jesus called his disciples to repent from their inflated egos. After John the Baptizer was put in prison, Jesus went up to Galilee and proclaimed, "The kingdom of God has come near. Repent and believe the good news!" (Mk. 1:15b). The apostle Peter, speaking to onlookers in the place called Solomon's Colonnade, near the temple in Jerusalem declared, "Repent, then, and turn to God, so that your sins may be wiped out, that times of refreshing may come from the Lord" (Acts 3:19a).[26] The call to repentance had continued for thousands of years. When there was no repentance, there was no forgiveness. A recurring call to live in repentance was commonly heard in the formative years of the ancient church, just as it should be heard today.

While repentance is essential to forgiveness and reconciliation, John Calvin, the prominent Reformation theologian, reminded us that our repentance does not earn God's forgiveness or love. In Book III of Calvin's *Institutes* he explained that repentance does not mean, "Repent, and if you repent you will be forgiven!" This statement

---

24. See Mark 6:12.
25. Also, see Mark 9:33-37.
26. Also see Acts: 2:38 and Acts 8:32.

was Calvin's summation of a distortion of the biblical teaching about forgiveness that became prevalent in the medieval sacrament of penance. Calvin argued that this teaching wrongly inverted the ancient church's understanding of the relationship between forgiveness and repentance by requiring repentance prior to grace and forgiveness. "It makes the imperatives of obedience prior to the indicatives of grace, and regards God's love and forgiveness and acceptance as conditional upon what we do—upon our meritorious acts of repentance." He was persuaded that the ancient understanding of repentance took this form: "Christ has borne your sins on the cross. Therefore, repent! Receive his forgiveness in repentance!" Repentance is our response to grace, not a condition of grace.[27] Clearly, while repentance is nonnegotiable, it is certainly not the precursor for forgiveness. Instead, it is the goodness of God that leads us directly to personal confession and repentance. Likewise, we extend the grace of forgiveness to others before their repentance is present, not as a consequence of (or reward for) repentance by those who hurt us.

If repentance is non-negotiable why then does God ask us to forgive persons who do not repent? The presence or absence of repentance really has no bearing on the universal call of God to forgive those who hurt us. We forgive because forgiveness liberates us from captivity to the actions of the other person. It also is an absolutely necessary element in our process of spiritual formation. Furthermore, we forgive in order to create an environment that can lead to the other person's repentance and ultimately to our reconciliation with them. While repentance is not a prerequisite for forgiveness, repentance is fundamental to meaningful reconciliation.

Repentance Is Ongoing

Repentance might start with a specific event in our lives, but it is an ongoing process, just as our forgiving of others is. The Old

---

27. James B. Torrance, *Worship, Community & The Triune God of Grace* (Downers Grove, IL: Intervarsity, 1996), 54-59. Quotes translated from Calvin's *Institutes* 3.4.

Testament prophet, Hosea (eighth century B.C.), wrote, "Return, Israel, to the LORD your God. Your sins have been your downfall! Take words[28] with you and return to the LORD. Say to him: Forgive all our sins and receive us graciously, that we may offer the fruit of our lips" (Hosea 14:1-2). Hosea records that Israel had fallen into sinful behavior, needed to change (repent from) their ways of living, and return to the Lord. Even though the word, repentance, is not used in the text, the call to repentance is blatant. From Hosea's use of the word 'return', we must infer that living in repentance is not a one time event. Hosea was speaking to those who knew God, whose lives had once been oriented to God. They had fallen into sin and needed to repent and return to their former way of life.

The need for on-going repentance is modeled by the apostle Peter. He had denied knowing Jesus three times after boldly declaring that he would never do so. When he remembered how Jesus had predicted that Peter would disown him, he wept bitterly.[29] His tears are evidence that repentance was being born his heart. Peter had been, and would again be a faithful follower of Jesus. His initial change of heart and behavior when he first chose to follow Jesus was not sufficient to cover all the things that would happen in the future. Like the rest of us, he faced a challenge to repent each time he saw his sins.

The secret to maintaining an ongoing heart of repentance is to live close to God through Jesus. Jesus said, "Remain in me, as I also remain in you. No branch can bear fruit by itself; it must remain in the vine. Neither can you bear much fruit unless you remain in me. I am the vine; you are the branches. If you remain in me and I in you, you will bear much fruit; apart from me you can do nothing" (John

---

28. *"Take words.* None could appear before the Lord empty-handed (Exod 23:15; 23:30), but animal sacrifices would not be enough. Only words of true repentance would be sufficient fruit of our lips" from the notes on verse 14:2 from the *Zondervan TNIV Study Bible* (Grand Rapids, MI: The Zondervan Corporation, 2006), 1487.

29. See Luke 22: 55-62.

15:4-5).[30] The metaphor of the vine pervades Jesus' relationship with the disciples. On the night when Jesus was later betrayed by one of his own disciples, he gathered with them to celebrate the Passover. At this last supper together, Jesus took the cup of wine and gave thanks and then said, "Take this and divide it among you. For I tell you I will not drink again of the fruit of the vine until the kingdom of God comes" (Luke 22:17-18). Shortly thereafter, he continued, "This cup is the new covenant in my blood, which is poured out for you" (Luke 22:20).

Jesus was sharing much more with his disciples than preparing them for what was to become of him. William Temple, Archbishop of Canterbury (1942-1944), points out that the image of the grape vine was the recognized symbol of Israel. All Jesus' disciples would have understood this imagery. The true vine stood for what Israel was called to be. Here Jesus proclaims that the purpose of God, entrusted to Israel, is now being fulfilled in himself. The image of the vine was clear, but Jesus' implication was startling. The vine lives to nourish the branches. The branches flower and bring forth the fruit of the vine. When the fruit is mature, and the vine has for a moment become glorious.[31] As Jesus makes explicit in John 15, God the Father is the gardener and Jesus is the vine, the one who supplies life to us who are the branches. Our life depends upon abiding in Jesus. To abide with anyone means we live with them in an ongoing relationship. It is in our relationship with God through Jesus that we are nurtured. The fruit that we bear comes to us through our connection to him.

This process is not the same as trying to live by the agendas of Christ, or striving to live by his ethics. To rely upon our best attempts at good behavior, rather than upon him personally, is to choose to walk apart from him. It is in such times of independence that we disrupt our heart of repentance. Yet, we are his, and we are invited

---

30. Also read the entire context of this teaching found in John 15:1-17.
31. William Temple, *Readings in St. John's Gospel* (First and Second Series), 252.

to return again to God through confession and repentance and draw our nourishment directly from him. We never reach a state of perfection where we no longer need a heart of ongoing repentance. To walk in repentance, we must experience the reality of knowing and enjoying ongoing fellowship with the triune God. Repentance remains in us as long as we live and abide in Christ.

John the Baptizer spoke to the crowds that came to be baptized, saying, "Produce fruit in keeping with repentance and do not begin to say to yourselves, 'We have Abraham as our father'" (Luke 3:8). It seems John anticipated that these newly baptized Jews would develop an entitlement mentality, thinking that they had a viable relationship with God based on their Jewish pedigree, rather than relying on repentance, which revealed itself through the fruit of God's Spirit in their life. Today, some of us might ignore our need to repent by concentrating instead on our Christian cultural heritage, our church membership, or the fact that we have been baptized. Others might focus on their many good accomplishments. Our wonderful deeds might well be a blessing to others, but they cannot substitute for a heart of ongoing repentance and a relationship to God through Jesus.

While this understanding offends the modern perspective, it was well-received by the ancient church, which left us records that emphasize the need for ongoing repentance. The *Apostolic Constitutions,* for example, are a collection of eight books probably put together by Clement of Rome in the late fourth century. In this account of liturgical practices and church policies, we see that repentance is neither a mindset alone, nor is it a one-time event.

> O bishop, just as you receive a pagan after you have
> instructed and baptized him, likewise let everyone
> join in prayers for this [penitent] man and restore
> him to his former place among the flock, through
> the imposition of hands. For he has been purified
> by repentance. And the imposition of hands shall

be similar to baptism for him. For, by the laying on
of hands, the Holy Spirit was given to believers.[32]

The purification discussed here is not that of a new con-
vert, but that of a baptized Christian who at some point after he was
baptized had returned to sinful behavior and then repented again.
Clement notes that the consequence of repentance is purification.
When contaminated water or metals are purified, impurities are
changed into a form that can then be removed. Purification leaves
the substance consistent throughout, with only the desired elements
present. As often as we return to activities that are incompatible with
God's purposes, purification is necessary. Ongoing repentance is the
means by which God removes what is inconsistent with godly character and our spiritual transformation.

Just as the ancient church affirmed the necessity of on-going
repentance, so, too, did leaders of the Protestant Reformation. Martin Luther was a sixteenth-century priest and theology professor at
a Roman Catholic seminary in Germany when he began wrestling
with the teaching of Scripture on many subjects, including repentance. He identified his objections to certain prevailing teachings
of the church, and then declared the Roman Church to be in error,
nailing his 95 theses of protest on the church door at Wittenberg in
1517.[33] Each of the 95 principles stood in opposition to the then current church teaching on crucial issues such as penances, indulgences
and the authority of the pope. Luther's theses stirred considerable
theological debate and are credited with launching what became
known as the Reformation. The first four of Luther's declarations
deal directly with repentance:

1. Our Lord and Master Jesus Christ, in saying, "Repent ye, etc.," meant the whole life of the faithful to
   be an act of repentance.

---

32. Clement of Rome, *Apostolic Constitutions* (Peabody, MA:
Hendrickson Publishers, 1994, c. 390, E) 7.415.
33. Martin Luther, *Documents of the Christian Church,* Henry
Bettenson and Chris Maunder, ed. (Oxford: Oxford University Press, 1949), 206.

2. This saying cannot be understood of the sacrament of penance (i.e. of confession and absolution), which is administered by the priesthood.

3. Yet he does not mean inner repentance only; nay, interior repentance is void if it does not externally produce different kinds of mortifications of the flesh.[34]

4. And so penance remains while self-hate remains (i.e. true interior penitence); namely right up to entrance into the kingdom of heaven.[35]

With these four points Luther proclaimed that for the Christian's entire life, he is to practice ongoing repentance until he draws his last breath. Contrary to the teaching of the Roman Church, Luther had come to believe that the humanly structured church could not dispense forgiveness on behalf of God. In contrast, he saw ongoing repentance as fundamental in the life of a Christian.

We have seen that Old Testament prophets and New Testament apostles, alike, taught us to maintain a lifestyle of ongoing repentance. Ancient Christian leaders and Christian reformers also affirmed our need to continue in repentance. Plainly, no one has ever reached a spiritual pinnacle where repentance is no longer needed, because none of us can reach perfection in our earthly life. Hear these words of Jesus: "If anyone would come after me, he must deny himself and take up his cross daily to follow me" (Luke 9:23). To deny one's self is not to classify everything that you enjoy as bad and then become miserable! Jesus does not tell us to take up his cross, which was suffering. Instead, he instructs each of us to take up our

---

34. By using the term that is translated in English as "mortifications of the flesh" Luther is referring to the death or cessation of actions that are sinful in nature. Interior repentance also must produce a fundamental change in our actions or we have not truly repented.

35. Luther knew nothing of the connotations these words have acquired in our day. He was stating that inward and outward levels of repentance were to be a part of our daily lives as long as we live on earth.

own cross and follow the will of God that is uniquely ours. To follow Christ requires that we stop seeking those things that displease God, and then constantly turn back to God in repentance. This is to be a daily process in which we reaffirm our allegiance to God with our mind, heart, and our behavior.

> *Seek the Lord while he may be found;*
> *call on him while he is near.*
>
> *Let the wicked forsake their ways*
> *and the unrighteous their thoughts.*
>
> *Let them turn to the Lord,*
> *and he will have mercy on them,*
>
> *And to our God, for he will freely pardon.*
> *"For my thoughts are not your thoughts,*
> *neither are your ways my ways."*
> —Isaiah 55:6-8

Chapter 9

Initiating Reconciliation

Ancient Understanding of Reconciliation

Conflict and the destruction of relationships are as old as recorded history. In the fourth chapter of Genesis, we learn of Cain, a farmer, who murdered his shepherd brother, Abel. Discord and animosity are present today in human relationships, just as they always have been. Each week most of us experience conflict with someone. We continually find ourselves in need of reconciliation, month after month.

Many things make reconciliation difficult. Our lack of diligence and our stubbornness, at times, create problems. When we make poor decisions, we accumulate trouble in our relationships. Our wrong choices sometimes victimize those who are innocent. People may try to align others against us. Sometimes we suffer for mistakes that others make. Hopefully, we welcome honest input from others, yet even those we trust do not always have accurate perceptions or reliable information. If we do not properly address conflicts, they can become long-term sources of stress for which we pay a high price. In the end, unresolved conflicts can result in everything from heartache to heart attacks.

Ultimately, all Christian spiritual formation can be traced back to God's desire for reconciliation. Because God desires all of his creation to be restored to its glory, he gave his Son to redeem it. All who believe in him, may be forgiven and reconciled.

But reconciliation is also work. Anyone who has ever reconciled a bank statement understands this. When we receive our monthly statements, we assemble our memories, check register entries, keypad entries from automated teller machines, and the transactions recorded by our banks. Each time we used our debit cards, write checks, or pay bills electronically, we became vulnerable to undesired stress. Each bank teller who processed a deposit could create a problem that will have to be reconciled. We must conduct a thorough, discerning, and relentless examination of our financial situation, identifying and correcting all errors, to determine how much money is really in our account. The longer we delay reconciliation of our account, the more complicated the task will become and the greater the problems that will arise. Reconciliation will be incomplete until every imperfection has been identified and accounted for and proper adjustments have been made to our records. Our bank statement is either reconciled or it is not—it is an absolute condition, not a relative condition.

When we are reconciling our bank account, our feelings have little role in discovering reality. When it comes to relationships, however, our feelings are the bedrock from which we assess reality. We know in our hearts the difference between a relationship that is severed and one that is connected. Almost everyone has experienced at some time the contrast between the pain of injury from a fractured friendship and the deep joy of reconciliation.

Reconciliation is not simply how we feel toward one another. We can be called to intervene and bring equilibrium to circumstances where suffering is present. We may be just the one to intervene and inject justice into a situation, where there has been injury, trauma, and suffering that we did not cause. We may need to speak out against practices that are inconsistent with the gospel. The apostle Paul was called back to Jerusalem by church leaders to defend his practice of forgoing circumcision among male Gentile converts.[1]

---

1. See Acts 15.

The other leaders of the church assumed that accepting Jesus as Messiah committed a Gentile to become a good Jew and be circumcised. Paul's strong defense of his reforming this ancient practice enabled reconciliation between new Gentile Christians and the Jerusalem leadership.

In the original Greek Scriptures, we find three distinct words that are translated by the English word 'reconcile'.[2] The first word used throughout the New Testament to denote reconciliation between humankind and God is *katallassō*. While the ancient Christians did not have on-line bank accounts as we have today, they used the word *katallassō* to refer to the change or exchange of something, especially money. This concept enabled them to understand the change from being God's enemies into being God's friends. That process begins when we change our attitude and accept the provision that God has made for us through Jesus Christ and are made right with God. We exchange our previous condition for a new one, one that has been given to us. This is by far the most prevalent understanding of the word reconciliation in the New Testament. The second word, *apokatallassō*, is sometimes (but not always) translated 'reconcile'.[3] It is essentially a stronger form of *katallassō*. Sometimes, it is translated as 'unity', suggesting that our relationships are to be in harmony, as opposed to discord.

The third word translated reconcile, *diallassō*, is used only once in the Scriptures, in Matthew 5:24.

> Therefore, if you are offering your gift at the altar and there remember that your brother or sister has something against you, leave your gift there in front of the altar. First go and be reconciled to that person; then come and offer your gift. (Matt 5:23-24)

---

2. See Vine, W. E. *Vine's Expository Dictionary of Old and New Testament Words* (Old Tappan, NJ: Fleming H. Revell Company, 1981), 260-262 for a detailed discussion of these words.

3. See Eph 1:10, 2:16, Phil 2:10, and Col 1:21-22.

Diallassō is used only to refer to the mending of relationships between two humans, never between humans and God. The meaning of this word is to affect a restoration in cases of mutual hostility. There is no such thing as mutual 'making up' where God and humankind are concerned because God is never hostile toward us. It is we who must be reconciled to God. But in relationships between people, there is a mutual responsibility to transform conflicted relationships into reconciled ones.

God's desire is that we live in reconciled relationships with him and with one another. The Gospel of Luke, chapter 15, records a striking picture of reconciliation. Although it is usually called the Parable of the Prodigal Son,[4] it is more accurately called the Parable of the Loving Father, for the hero in the story is the father, not the son. The word 'reconcile' is not used in the passage, but the entire parable concerns reconciliation. Jesus tells the story of a wayward young man who asked to receive his inheritance prior to his father's death. His father consents and his son squanders it all in 'wild living'. Having exhausted his inheritance, the young man sinks so far into poverty and that he accepts a job feeding pigs, and longs to eat what the pigs are given. This would have been particularly degrading, not only because of what the hogs were fed, but also because feeding pigs was specifically forbidden. Jewish law stated, "Cursed is he who feeds swine."[5]

Religious people would have not hesitated to condemn the young man for mistreating his father and for allowing himself to get into these circumstances. At this point in the story the young man realizes that he has made foolish choices. Recognizing that he is no longer worthy to receive even his father's love, he decides to return home and beg to be taken in as a hired servant, a position that would place him, culturally, beneath his father's slaves. In the Jewish culture, slaves were in some remote sense a permanent part of the family, but

---

4. See Luke 15:11-32.

5. William Barclay, *The Gospel of Luke, Revised Edition* (Philadelphia, PA: The Westminster Press, 1975), 204.

a hired servant was more akin to a day laborer, who could be dismissed with no notice by the master of the house when his services were no longer needed. Yet, while this prodigal was still a speck on the horizon, his father, who must have been peering hopefully down the road, sees him coming. The father is so excited to see him that, without regard for his own dignity or his ill treatment at his son's hands and before hearing so much as a word from his self-centered, rebellious son's lips, he runs down the road to embrace him. After this incredible greeting, the son confesses his self-centered ways and as he had planned, declares that he is not worthy to be called a son. But the father completely ignores his son's protests of unworthiness. Instead, he lavishes his son with gifts and then orders that a feast be prepared to celebrate his son's return to life with the family out of virtual death. The father's actions plainly declare that despite his knowledge of his son's behavior, he has always loved his son. The younger son's acknowledgment of his destructive ways, his hope in his father's mercy, and the son's willingness to gratefully receive the lowest social position in his father's household reveal his unconditional repentance. His change of heart, confession, and return allow him to comprehend and experience the father's unconditional love, which had always been available.

Jesus goes on to say that during his younger brother's absence, the older son had remained at home continuing to do all his assigned tasks. Hearing the loud music, he asks one of the servants what is going on. When he learns that his father is honoring his brother, he is furious. Unmoved by his brother's return, and jealous of the attention his brother is receiving, he complains to his father: there had been no parties for him.

There are many lessons to be learned from this parable, but we will look at only a few of them. Jesus paints a picture of God the Father as loving and welcoming. We have all been the wayward children of God at some point in our lives, and God's love precedes us on our journey back to God. If we fail to turn from self-destruction and isolation and return to our Heavenly Father, we cannot experience his love or live in his presence. But as the story progresses, we clearly see that full reconciliation is possible. While the son was away living a wasteful and self-indulgent life, he recognized the great poverty in which he was living. No doubt he realized in his heart that his father had not ceased to love him (confessed). The son acknowledged (confessed) and left the destructive, self-centered lifestyle (repented) which eventually left him in financial ruins and emotional isolation and returned home to his family, trusting in his father's faithfulness. The father organizes the celebration party for his son's homecoming and accepts him back as his son, not a hired servant. As we confess the truth and turn from our destructive ways, our hearts fill with love and appreciation for God's initiating love. We now enjoy with God the unique fellowship and unity of heart that exists between a loving parent and child. Our relationship with God is back in balance—reconciled.

The insights from Jesus' story do not end there, because there are two sons. The older son's resentment of his brother is obvious. When he confronts his father, the older son refers to his younger brother, not as 'my brother', but as 'your son'.[6] And while the details of the younger son's sins are unknown, his older brother cleverly ascribes to him the squandering of the property on prostitutes. Although the older son was entitled by Jewish law to receive twice the assets his younger brother received,[7] he appears to resent that his younger brother returned home to consume a portion of what was his inheritance. Both sons rejected their father's love, but we only know for certain that one repented.

Like older brothers who have never journeyed away from home, those who strive to remain faithful to God must transcend resentment and judgments against those who have abandoned the

---

6. This phrase brings to mind the many times I have heard a former spouse referred to as 'my ex', 'the kids' dad', or 'the kids' mom'. I infer that this attempt to depersonalize a former spouse reveals a great wound that probably has not yet had the benefit of complete forgiveness.

7. Taken from Jewish law which governed rules of inheritance, found in Deut 21:17 and Bamidar 27:5-11 from the Torah.

household of God, whether the 'prodigals' have yet returned or not. Our judgments stem from an erroneous presumption that our good behavior places us closer to God's heart. Such is never the case. Our joy in the experience of being with our Heavenly Father ought to increase, not diminish when someone else returns to God.

We might see ourselves as either the younger or the older brother or perhaps at times some of both. Yet the true model for us is the father. This man loved both of his sons. No doubt, he was grieved by his younger son's premature departure from the household and by the life that his younger son chose, yet this father's love was undiminished. The moment he saw his son retuning, he ran to welcome him home. There was no judgment in the father's heart—only great joy because the one he loved had returned to enjoy being with him. The power to love unconditionally, as the father loves, is possible for us when we live in a close relationship with God. Then we are able to anticipate reconciliation and remain vigilant to welcome any who have hurt us as they make the attempt to return into our lives. We forgive, though we do not excuse bad decisions, wasting of precious resources, and personal rejection, even when they have broken our heart. We recognize that we are not responsible for any person's decisions, nor is it our role to pronounce punishment against them. Instead, we greet them with the love of the father.

Luke chapter 15 contains two additional parables that illustrate the great joy God has when one who has been lost is found. Jesus tells a story about a shepherd who has lost a single sheep. He leaves his herd of ninety-nine sheep to go and rescue the stray. The final parable is about a woman who loses one of her ten valuable coins. When she finds the missing coin, she calls her neighbors and friends and asks them to rejoice with her. These stories of the lost son, the lost sheep, and the lost coin speak to the way God longs for every person who is not close to him. God has great joy when we are reconciled with him. The example of God challenges us to sustained reconciliation in all our relationships.

Reconciliation Transforms Conflicts into Unity

The contemporary worldview has confused the terms reconciliation, unity, and tolerance. Reconciliation is often equated with being willing to 'get along' even though we totally disagree on a matter. Unity is sometimes reframed to be the absence of hostility. This understanding is as fulfilling as believing that the absence of hate toward someone is the same thing as loving them. The ancient understanding of reconciliation and unity was not polite, peaceful co-existence. It was not a denial on anyone's part of what had happened in conflict. Reconciliation meant that where there had once been hurt, there was now a restored, interactive relationship. Unity, like the other aspects of forgiveness, is expressed outwardly by our actions, but it is not merely an action. Neither is it merely cerebral or emotional, even though we can have great relief and a feeling of connectedness as a result of living in unity. Unity originates from within our deepest self and is based on the truth.

Unity is often incorrectly identified with uniformity—sameness. The contemporary church seems to promote conformity more often than genuine unity. Demanding sameness undermines the reality of both reconciliation and unity as was experienced by the ancient Christians. True unity actually *requires* differences and distinctions. For example, a single musical voice can be beautiful as can ten persons singing the same melody line in unison (sameness). But when multiple voices, singing at different pitches and rhythms, are combined into one harmonious choral work, you then have magnificent unity. Relatively malleable gold is combined with harder metals so it can be molded into jewelry that is not pliable. Gravel is mixed with wet cement so that the resulting concrete will be solid and durable. A fundamental principle of unity is that elements that differ are combined to produce an outcome greater than the sum of the individual parts.

The early Christians believed that God's gathering of the diverse peoples of the earth into one unified church is similar to the gathering of different grains, from different stalks of wheat and different fields, tended by different farmers in varying ways and traditions to make bread. But the grains were gathered together and changed into something better with common hands by someone who had an intended purpose for their change through an intentional process. The image of a diversity of grains of wheat brought together to make the one loaf stands in contrast with so many of our Christian communities today, where sameness has eclipsed unity. The image of unity is clearly presented by *The Didache* in the following prayer, used at the celebration of Christian Communion during the first century:

> Regarding the Eucharist. Give thanks as follows: "We give Thee thanks, Our Father, for the Holy Vine of David Thy servant, which Thou hast made known to us through Jesus, Thy servant. To Thee be glory for evermore." Next, concerning the broken bread: "We give Thee thanks, Our Father, for the life and knowledge which Thou hast made known to us through Jesus, Thy servant. To Thee be the glory for evermore. As this broken bread was scattered over the hills and then, when gathered, became one mass, so may Thy Church be gathered from the ends of the earth into Thy Kingdom. For Thine is the glory and the power through Jesus Christ for evermore."[8]

In this ancient prayer, it is clear that both the bread and the church are being transformed into something greater than the sum of their parts. Reconciliation and unity are fashioned out of diversity.

This excerpt from a contemporary liturgy uses similar imagery and was possibly inspired by the prayer above.

> Send your Holy Spirit upon us, we pray, that the sharing of the bread we break and the cup that we bless may be for us the communion of the body and blood of Christ. Grant that, being joined together

8. James A. Kleist, S.J., Ph.D., translator, Didache 9:1-4, from *Ancient Christian Writers*, vol. 6 (New York, NY: The Newman Press, 1948), 20.

in him, we may attain to the unity of the faith and
grow up in all things into Christ, our Lord. And as
this grain has been gathered from many fields into
one loaf, and these grapes form many hills into
one cup, grant, O Lord, that your whole church
may soon be gathered from the ends of the earth
into your kingdom. Even so, come, Lord Jesus![9]

Here, we see the added image of the vine—the holy vine of
David, the ongoing understanding that Jesus is God's provision for
their spiritual nourishment. Reconciliation and the ensuing unity
are not based on being like one another, but on liking and loving one
another and sharing together a common life with God. The prayer
emphasizes our reconciliation with God and one another through
Christ. It petitions God to bring us to maturity and our unity into
full reality.

As these prayers suggest, the hallmark of the germinal Christian church was not beautiful buildings, great choral literature or
ornate vestments; it was not popular styled praise choruses, perfectly
staged drama, or high-definition video presentations. It was not even
great Bible preaching since the New Testament was not compiled for
a number of years after the establishment of the church. Worship
was low-tech and low luxe. The hallmark of the ancient Christian
was the unity of heart between those within the community of God.

From the beginning, Christians made being together a pri-
ority.[10] They knew one another. They knew God and shared in their
experience of reconciliation with one another, despite significant differences. Some early Christians were rich and many were poor, but
their bond of unity was so strong that their lives and possessions
were voluntarily available to help those among them who were in
need.[11] The unity they shared in their common life was through Jesus
Christ—and nothing else. Paul wrote to the Galatians, "You are all

---

9. *Reformed Church in America General Synod, Order of Worship: The
Lord's Day,* Reformed Church Press, (quoted from *The Worship Sourcebook,* 324).
   10. See Heb 10:24-25.
   11. See Acts 4:32-35.

sons of God through faith in Christ Jesus, for all of you who were baptized into Christ have clothed yourselves with Christ. There is neither Jew nor Greek, slave nor free, male nor female, for you are all one in Christ Jesus" (Gal 3:26-28).

The early church was shaped by the religious and cultural values of the Jewish people. Because the Jews had a strong grasp of God's historic provision for them, the initial converts to Christianity also perceived God as their provider and source of life. The Jews, while of many diverse opinions, were unified by many centuries of common suffering and their trust in God. Their unity is evident through their shared, celebrated remembrances of God's protection for them. For example, the Jewish prayer before meals would not ask God to bless the food, but would express their desire to bless God with their thanksgiving and praise for his provision for them. Consequently, the first Christians had a strong sense of connection. Drawing on this Jewish background, the first Christians crafted their worship services to express their unity in God through Christ calling them Eucharists, or thanksgivings.

To see such unity among his followers was the parting wish of Jesus. Following his last supper with his disciples, Jesus went to a garden and prayed to his Heavenly Father:

> My prayer is not for them alone. I pray also for those
> who will believe in me through their message, that
> all of them may be one, Father, just as you are in
> me and I am in you. May they also be in us so that
> the world may believe that you have sent me. I have
> given them the glory that you gave me, that they may
> be one as we are one—I in them and you in me—so
> that they may be brought to complete unity. Then
> the world will know that you sent me and have loved
> them even as you have loved me. (John 17:20-23)

Jesus desired that his followers would live in unity with one another in the same way that Jesus lived in unity with his Father. He did not pray that everyone would believe the right doctrine, or be the same, or do the same things. His prayer was that all his disciples, including those in the coming generations, would be unified in love for one another and in the mission of reconciliation, which he and his Father had begun.

Early Christians looked to God to establish their unity rather than striving for it by conformity in actions. They understood that forgiveness that led to reconciliation could not be earned by their best attempts at obedience. While they were called to obedience, it never meant simply external compliance, but was always viewed as a matter of one's heart and will. The consequence of a reconciled Christian community is unity established through Christ. When we are in union with Christ, we are in union with one another. When we are joined to Christ, we are joined to one another.

Ambassadors for Reconciliation

Jesus' bold, missional exhortation, known as the Great Commission, is "go and make disciples of nations, baptizing them in the name of the Father and of the Son and of the Holy Spirit, and teaching them to obey everything I have commanded you. And surely I am with you always to the very end of the age" (Matt 28:19-20). The word translated 'nations' in English is the Greek word *ethnē* from which we derive the words 'ethnic' and 'ethos', concepts which communicate the scope of Jesus' meaning more accurately than 'nations'. The community of the Christian church is to be a unique union of diverse people. God desires disciples from all races, all levels of education and economic strata, and all cultures to be reconciled in his Son.

The apostle Paul proclaimed clearly that reconciliation is God's primary motive:

> Therefore, if anyone is in Christ, the new creation has
> come; the old has gone, the new has come! All this
> is from God, who reconciled us to himself through
> Christ and gave us the ministry of reconciliation: that
> God was reconciling the world to himself in Christ, not

counting men's sins against them. And he has committed to us the message of reconciliation. We are therefore Christ's ambassadors, as though God were making his appeal through us. We implore you on Christ's behalf: Be reconciled to God. God made him who had no sin to be sin for us, so that in him we might become the righteousness of God. (2 Cor 5:17-21)

Once we are united with God, we are appointed as ambassadors for Christ. An ambassador who is resident in an alien country represents his home country to the foreign government. Ambassadors must understand and be committed to the interests of their own country, while effectively communicating with the leadership and citizens of another country to which he has been assigned. We are exhorted to be reconciled with God and become ambassadors of reconciliation with one another. The call to reconciliation with God cannot be separated from the call to be agents of reconciliation with one another.

Unfortunately, many Christians live in isolation from one another and from those who are not followers of Christ. Our isolationist lifestyles make us inadequate ambassadors for reconciliation. Too many Christians drive miles to attend church or soccer practice, but do not know the names of the children or elderly people who live next door to them. It does not occur to us to get to know them, because we have such full schedules. We take a passive stance, failing to initiate new, connected relationships or pursue reconciliation in established relationships. Isolationism rejects Jesus' command of "go and make disciples" (Matt 28:19). He does not say to make converts, church members, or notches on our spiritual gun-handles. We are appointed to make disciples—that is followers of Christ. Certainly that process starts with the making of friends whom we learn to know and love.

As Christ's ambassadors, Christians are to change their behavior enthusiastically to redeem broken relationships. Reconciliation can come about only by working through the processes of forgiveness, confession, and repentance. To attempt reconciliation with God or with one another, without moving through these spiritual antecedent processes will produce a counterfeit and short-lived shadow of reconciliation. When we bypass these important steps, we are really redesigning God's process. If we leave out confession and repentance, we deny the reality of our sin and we exhibit our arrogance in the mistaken belief that we know better than God how to bring about reconciliation. This contra-Christ agenda undermines the reputation of Jesus. It obscures the clarity of the truth that he has chosen and drawn us to himself.

Our shopping malls, sports arenas, academic institutions, and corporate cultures are filled with people who futilely promote alternative ideas of self-sufficiency. Some of our churches and seminaries that identify themselves as Christian promote alternatives by denying humanity's sinful nature or by the promotion and perpetuation of images of self-deprecation, as if being human was fundamentally deficient. These dis-unifying innovations often place conditions upon forgiveness and reconciliation that we are tempted to embrace. When true confession and unquestionable repentance occur, reconciliation and unity will follow as the natural consequence.

An ongoing lifestyle of forgiveness and reconciliation is a necessary attribute of our ambassadorship, for we cannot serve as effective ambassadors for something that we do not know personally. Thus, each of us needs to be reconciled to God—Father, Son, and Holy Spirit—and with one another. Our thankful response to God's unconditional and universal offer of forgiveness begets such reconciliation. The apostle Paul summarized the means of reconciliation in his letter to the Christians in Rome:

> For if, when we were God's enemies, we were reconciled to him through the death of his Son, how much more, having been reconciled, shall we be saved through his life! Not only is this so, but we also boast in God through our Lord Jesus Christ, through whom we have now received reconciliation. (Rom 5:10-11)

These words to the Roman Christians stress God's attitude of favor toward us. Although our relationship with God hinges upon our acceptance of God's gift, the Scriptures affirm that God never changes his attitude of love toward us.[12] The prophet Malachi states, "I the Lord do not change" (Mal 3: 6). The apostle James affirms, "Every good and perfect gift is from above, coming down from the Father of the heavenly lights, who does not change like shifting shadows" (Jas 1:17). The unchangeableness of God is also mirrored by the apostle Paul who wrote, "Jesus Christ is the same yesterday and today and forever" (Heb 13:8). God's character—his righteousness and loving kindness—is changeless. This characteristic of God guarantees that we can receive reconciliation and live in unity together. The death of his Son is the means by which God has won the cosmic war against evil and is now in the process of reconciling all of his creation to himself. Our mission of mercy as an ambassador is to help others to come to grips with the reality of this truth in their own lives.

> *How good and pleasant it is when*
> *God's people live together in unity!*
> —Psalm 133:1

---

12. While Scripture affirms that God can and has changed his mind on certain actions he might take, Scriptural references to God as unchangeable refer to his character and his loving initiatives with us.

Chapter 10

Opportunities to Reclaim Transformational Forgiveness

No Magical Formulas Exist

Our path to reconciliation cannot be set by a sequence of events in a flow-chart. There is no magical formula or astute logical process that will guarantee the outcome we desire. Most of us have learned by now that reliance upon a formula will not ensure the answer to prayer we desire, an end to cruel international conflict, or a supernatural healing of our loved one. Neither can a formula guarantee that the one who has hurt us will seek our forgiveness or that we will enjoy reconciliation. While it is tempting to offer a cookbook approach to transformational forgiveness, this would be contrary to the gospel and to reality.

Clearly, there are many facets of the forgiveness-reconciliation process. Constructing a formula to encompass them all would, indeed, be a demanding task. Those who highly value the Scriptures might begin by compiling an exhaustive list of the verses that address how we are to be reconciled with God. The list would include such phrases as, "repent and be baptized,"[1] "believe in the Lord Jesus,"[2] "declare with your mouth, 'Jesus is Lord,' and believe in your heart that God raised him from the dead,"[3] and "confess your sins to each

---

1. See Acts 2:38.
2. See Acts 16:31.
3. See Rom 10:9.

other and pray for each other."[4] A person might then try to derive a broadly based formula, covering all the listed elements. Most of us are not that exhaustive. More often than not, Christians construct a formula by simply hand-selecting satisfying verses from Scripture, which justify their personal opinions about forgiveness and reconciliation. We ride these verses like hobby horses to distinguish our theology from those who rely upon other Scripture verses for a different formula.

Some, perhaps not so scripturally minded, try to discern a formula based on experience or emotion. Such formulas might include retaliation until the offender complies with our demands for a truce. While this particular formula might bring about submission by some, its use will not result in reconciliation.

Implicit in any formula is the assumption that once we have perceived a profitable procedure, all we need to do is perform the prescribed tasks in the formula to receive the outcome we want. Such an approach, while intended to give concrete assistance in difficult situations, easily misses the essence of forgiveness and reconciliation at the center of God's heart. The existence of a formula inevitably induces us to measure one another's performance by that formula. Whatever formula you or I might decide to use, you can rest assured that someone else will be using a different one! Putting our trust in formulas—especially theological ones—blinds us to what God desires to do and leads us away from how God desires us to live. Our empowerment for forgiveness always comes from God, never from a carefully executed game plan. The writer of Proverbs summed up this wisdom when he wrote, "Trust in the Lord with all your heart and lean not unto your own understanding. In all your ways submit to him and he will make your paths straight [or direct your path]" (Prov 3:5-6).

Our task is not an activity we do which then produces our transformation. Our principal action is to rely upon God's

---

4. See Jas 5:16.

faithfulness and acknowledge his ability to bring about transformation in the timeframe that he chooses. This act of worship is the key to our transformation whether we are hoping for a restoration of our relationship with him or with another person. All action we take must be subordinate to relying on God's faithful action on our behalf. The process described in this book is not a formula but God's dynamic design for restoring relationships. By God's design we have a need to recognize and take responsibility for our actions. In confession we are drawn to agree with God's point of view as well as the point of view of those whom we have hurt. Our minds, hearts, and behavior change, and then we repent. The result of this process is reconciliation with God and with one another.

In the ancient church, new believers reoriented themselves toward trusting God, and after their changed hearts and character had been affirmed by the Christian community, they could anticipate their baptism. Like they, we experience ongoing Christian transformation by living out of a sense of the significance of our baptism into Christ. As a consequence of walking with God, we experience reconciliation and unity with others. This way of life stands in stark contrast to the way of living promoted by those who live out of a sense of obligation and fear of displeasing God. Those who take that path never reach genuine reconciliation with those with whom they have conflict.

A transformation process that culminates in reconciliation need not occur in any particular sequence. People respond to God's prompting and enter a life of reconciliation in many different ways. It is crucial only that our hearts be changed so that we respond in love to those who have hurt us and approach in great humility those whom we have offended. In the same manner that God approaches us, we are called to offer unconditional forgiveness to those who hurt and grieve us. As we forgive those who hurt us, these persons also make a choice whether or not to accept the forgiveness we offer. Lasting transformation begins in our hearts and, in turn, motivates us to change our behavior, not the other way around.

Ready for Launch

On July 16, 1969, the historic launch of Apollo 11 carried three courageous astronauts away from launch pad 39-A at Cape Canaveral, Florida. For these astronauts, this journey was unique. Although all three had previously flown in space on separate missions, this first trip together would break new ground in space exploration. In preparation for their historic mission, astronauts Neil Armstrong, Buzz Aldrin, and Michael Collins had trained endlessly. They knew what they were to do in both expected and unexpected situations. They were a unified community, a team that knew how to work well together to accomplish their mission despite their differences, individual personal aspirations, and unique roles in the mission. Like every astronaut, they were well aware that they were dependent on the data, observations, knowledge, and experience of many others. They relied on the powerful support structure at NASA and the scientists and fellow astronauts in Houston who provided guidance and wisdom throughout their flight.

Space exploration is and always will be replete with danger. Fewer than three years earlier three astronauts had died when a fire broke out in their cockpit right on the launch pad. Like every launch, the launch of Apollo 11 was a moment of great risk. The powerful Saturn V rocket had been successfully launched on five previous occasions, but those successes provided no guarantee of success this time. In flight engines had to fire or reignite precisely on schedule in order for their craft to safely reach the moon, maintain orbit, descend to and return from the lunar surface, and then return safely to earth. The slightest error or breakdown would lead to a crisis. The astronauts were never far away from life-threatening danger through their entire voyage.

The most dangerous moments of a flight are during the execution of new and unproven procedures. On the Apollo 11 mission the descent to the lunar surface, the actual human exploration of the lunar surface, and the ascent of the lunar module back to rejoin the command ship were all new adventures. Though these activities had been thoroughly designed and planned out, they had yet to be experienced. Nevertheless, Armstrong, Aldrin, and Collins were eager to step outside the comfortable box of the familiar in order to live new transformational experiences. Their experience would be possible only if they left the safety of Earth and placed themselves in a hostile, life-threatening environment. And then, only after they successfully left the relative safety of the command module, descended, and landed on the lunar surface could Armstrong and Aldrin begin to experience the excitement of the lunar surface. While his two colleagues were conducting planned experiments on the lunar surface, Command Module Pilot Michael Collins anxiously circled the moon time after time, alone in the command craft faithfully protecting the only craft that could return the three of them to earth at the appointed time.

All three astronauts had imagined and studied what it would be like to be a part of the first crew to land upon the moon. Because they received excellent education and endured countless practice sessions, they had faith that their venture would become reality, despite the fact that no one had made this journey before. Now, they would experience this reality first-hand.

For those of us back on planet Earth, who witnessed these events first-hand, the experiences were thrilling. Millions of us watched the first human contact with the lunar surface on live television. We stayed up late at night and adjusted our black and white television sets to optimize the snowy picture so we could see and hear every detail as it happened live from the moon. We sensed that in the small, remote NASA community faithful individuals were carrying out their roles so that we millions of others could witness what had seemed utterly impossible only a decade earlier. We felt that nothing would ever be the same now that humankind had walked on the surface of the another celestial body—the moon.

This trip did not invent the reality of the moon, nor was it the beginning of discoveries about the moon, but was a culmination of human knowledge regarding the moon. The trip made history because three men journeyed into the unfamiliar based on a course charted out for them by those who knew more than they did. This unparalleled adventure transformed an imaginary fantasy into an objective reality.

Just as great courage was required for these astronauts to venture into unfamiliar territory, it takes courageous people to venture into the unfamiliar landscape of forgiveness. To forgive unconditionally those who have caused us pain is to risk being deeply wounded if our efforts at reconciliation come to nothing. The deeper the wound, the harder it will be to forgive someone. It will be especially difficult for those who do not have many friends who understand the realities of transformational forgiveness. Despite all this, we take the risk because it is what we are called to be and do.

In order for us to take the risk to forgive, there are several important prerequisites. First, we must have a vision of something new. We must want inner freedom more than we fear being hurt. We must approach forgiveness with the perspective of Neil Armstrong, Edwin Aldrin, and Michael Collins. We need humility and proper objective knowledge. We must be willing to depend on reliable, outside resources for insight and guidance. We need the courage to leap out of our personal comfort zones, and attempt something extraordinary. We must have a personal willingness and the commitment to live out the truth each time we face the undesired world of shattered relationships. We must take these risks in order to be transformed. Living like this is not safe, but it is good.

We must know the ancient wisdom about forgiveness in the same way that the astronauts knew their spacecraft and the surface of the moon. Knowing *about* them will never be enough. I am not talking about memorizing the flight manual, but about the experience of sitting at the controls of the spacecraft and seeing what happens when we maneuver it to the intended destination and back to earth.

In English the word 'know' has at least two distinct meanings. We can know the facts about events and people on an intellectual level. We know what happened in Western civilization in the years of 1492, 1776, and on December 7, 1941. But cognitive knowledge alone, however factually accurate, will never enable us to understand, receive, or give forgiveness. These necessary verbal descriptions of transformational forgiveness must not remain mere words in our heads. Great words are only the starting point for our discoveries. The type of 'knowing' we need comes from walking through the personal experience of forgiveness.

I am reminded of a scene in the movie entitled *Good Will Hunting*. The title character, Will, is sitting on a park bench talking to his court-appointed therapist, when the therapist says, "Will, if I asked you about art, you could probably give me all the skinny on every art book ever written. Michelangelo—you know a lot about him, his life work, political aspirations, sexual orientation. But I bet you can't tell me what it smells like in the Sistine Chapel. You have never actually stood there and looked up at that beautiful ceiling, because you have never been out of Boston!"[5] We must all get out of Boston and let forgiveness that we describe with words become a reality which consumes our hearts. To launch into living this way is to be transformed.

The Shift into Postmodernity

Every culture in the world has its own metanarrative. A metanarrative is the master story of knowledge. It is the big story or lens through which all other observations and interpretations are made regarding the world.[6] Two thousand years ago, Christians thought of themselves as living in God's story. Today we are more likely to live in our own stories. Our new metanarrative has put us at the center. We are no longer theocentric but anthropocentric. This is a consequence of our shift to a postmodern worldview.

---

5. This is the author's condensation of the therapist's exhortation to Will from the movie, *Good Will Hunting*, (Miramax Films, 1997).

6. For an excellent resource see *Who Gets to Narrate the World?* by Robert E. Webber (Downers Grove, IL: InterVarsity Press, 2008).

Postmodernists say that meaning can be determined only from within an 'interpretive community'. They see reason and language as intrinsically deceptive sources of knowledge. However, Christians, while recognizing that an exclusive dependence upon reason is flawed, do believe in absolute truths. God reveals himself through language, and language is capable of expressing truth and universal values.

In the postmodern worldview, objective singular truth does not exist.[7] Thus, your truth is true for you and my truth is true for me. Even if our two truths seem mutually exclusive, we need not feel anxious, because we all realize that different metanarratives are of equal merit. One can find an ancient definition of postmodernity in the Scriptures: "everyone did what was right in his own eyes" (Judg 21:24 NKJV). Those of us who dissent from this postmodernist mindset are often labeled 'intolerant' for claiming that there is only one truth. For the postmodernist, the claims of Christianity are not denied; they are rejected *because* they purport to be true. On matters concerning forgiveness, Christians must stand against postmodern relativism. The reality is that we are reconciled to God through Christ alone and through God's initiative, not our own. Robert Webber explains,

> The biblical God is an active God—he creates, becomes active in the world to rescue his creation from sin and death, and restores the world to paradise and beyond in the new heavens and new earth. The centerpiece of his saving action is the Incarnation, death, and resurrection, where sin and death have been defeated and where the deliverance of creatures and creation, which will be consummated at the end of history, will begin. In the meantime, worship is a witness to this vision.[8]

---

7. Robert E. Webber, *Ancient-Future Faith: Rethinking Evangelicalism for a Postmodern World* (Grand Rapids, MI: Baker Books, 1999), 95.
8. Robert E. Webber, *Ancient-Future Worship: Proclaiming and Enacting God's Narrative* (Grand Rapids MI: Baker Books, 2008), 66.

The humility that is required for us to confess God's point of view about our sin and to confess to those we hurt by our own actions is demonstrated through the life and death of Jesus. He took the form of a servant, starting with his Incarnation and ending in his death on the cross, all the while forgiving those who were putting him to death.

Though it is difficult for anyone to embrace a life that mirrors the humility of Jesus, those with a postmodern, relativistic view must overcome more. Postmodern relativism provides a justification for preserving self-interest and orchestrating how and when to forgive someone. Consequently, those with a postmodern view are even more likely to want to establish the terms under which they will need, give, and receive forgiveness. Despite our firm rejection of relativism, there are aspects of postmodernity that Christians can and should embrace. In the postmodern framework, the critical social unit is the community rather than the individual. In order to reach people with the news of God's forgiveness in Christ, Christians need to create forgiving communities where people can be nurtured in the faith. The reality of a postmodern world is that people will come to faith not because they comprehend the logic of the argument, but because they have experienced a welcoming God in a hospitable and loving community.[9] The forgiving Christian community and its life in the world is becoming the new apologetic. To combat the errors of postmodernism Christians must provide an alternative 'interpretive community'. Promoting communities where forgiveness and forbearance are extended, rather than judgment and condemnation, will strike at the very core of the postmodern culture.

We Can Respond in a Different Way

Perhaps the sort of forgiveness and reconciliation I am describing seems utopian and impossible, beyond the capacity of

---

9. Robert E. Webber, *Ancient-Future Faith: Rethinking Evangelicalism for a Postmodern World.* (Grand Rapids, MI: Baker Books, 1999), 70-71.

flesh and blood human beings. Left to our own devices, forgiveness and reconciliation are, indeed, impossible.

In the twelfth chapter of his letter to the church at Rome, written at least in part to resolve disunity between Jewish and Gentile Christians, the apostle Paul offers a way forward writing, "Do not conform to the pattern of this world, but be transformed by the renewing of your mind. Then you will be able to test and approve what God's will is—his good, pleasing and perfect will" (Rom 12:2).

Many Christians mistakenly believe that this exhortation is intended to require proper moralistic behavior. This is not the case. Paul's point is to explain the means by which we can live our lives in total dedication to God. God has far more in mind than promoting the avoidance of sexual impurity, overeating, and smoking! To be "transformed by the renewing of your mind" is to understand reality from God's point of view. Paul recommends this paradigm shift, which promises not only to transform a person's inner world, but also to lead to unified and harmonious relationships. In such circumstances our ability to wisely and properly discern God's will is assured. Disputes and division will continue to surface within the Christian community, but mature Christians will no longer ignore them. They will know God's will and take the initiative to bring about reconciliation.

Recent history provides us with several powerful examples of people whose relationships have been transformed by forgiveness.

Corrie ten Boom's family members were among the "righteous Gentiles"[10] who risked their lives to save Jewish refugees in Holland, during World War II. After their arrest by the Gestapo, she and her sister, Betsie, were imprisoned in the Ravensbruck concentration camp. Their incarceration included an eleven-hour workday,

---

10. In 1967 Corrie ten Boom was honored as one of the "Righteous among the Nations" by the State of Israel. This is the highest award by the government to non-Jews who assisted and protected Jews during World War II. This award is administered by Yad Vashem, the authority in Israel commissioned to help remember the Holocaust. See http://www1.yadvashem.org/heb_site/righteous/pdf/virtual_wall_of_honor/NETHERLANDS.pdf, accessed July 5, 2009.

terrible working conditions, meager food rations, flea-infested sleeping conditions, and inadequate medical care. During the months in the camp, Betsie became sick and eventually died in December 1944 just three days before Corrie learned that she would be released. Corrie lost not only her sister to the Nazis, but her aged father and a favorite nephew. Then, in 1947 at a church in Munich, she encountered a man whom she recognized as one of the cruelest guards at Ravensbruck. He had since become a Christian, and was certain that God had forgiven him, but he was not certain that Corrie would. After struggling with great hatred, she knew that she must forgive him, yet felt only coldness in her heart. She prayed for Jesus to help her, and then she recalled, "woodenly, mechanically, I thrust out my hand into the one stretched out to me…. And then this healing warmth seemed to flood my whole being, bringing tears to my eyes."[11] Amazingly, she was able then to respond to him saying, "I forgive you brother, with all my heart."[12]

Elisabeth Elliot was a Christian missionary to Ecuador in the 1950s. Her husband Jim had always hoped to take the gospel to an unreached, secluded tribe. The Ecuadorian Aucas were such a group, with a fierce reputation for killing all who tried to contact them. Jim and four other missionaries successfully entered the area where the Aucas lived. Following what appeared to be a friendly contact with three of the Aucas, all five missionaries were speared to death. Elisabeth chose to stay in Ecuador as a missionary and within a year or two, fortuitously met two women from this tribe whom she befriended. This led her to live among the Aucas for two years. She not only forgave the Aucas for killing her husband and the other four missionaries, but she shared God's love with them on a daily

---

11. Corrie ten Boom, *Tramp for the Lord* (Old Tappan, NJ: Fleming H. Revel Company, 1974), 57.

12. Geoffrey Hanks, "Corrie ten Boom" from Seventy Great Christians, see http://www.geocities.com/Wellesley/7514/cory.html?20091 accessed February 1, 2009.

basis. The story of the Elliots is documented in her powerful book, *Through Gates of Splendor.*[13]

Nelson Mandela led the struggle against South African apartheid as a political activist and leader in the African National Congress. He was convicted of treason in 1964 and sentenced to life in prison. After he had served twenty-six years of captivity, international pressure led to his release in 1990. In 1994, he became the first president of the post-apartheid South Africa. He authorized South Africa's Truth and Reconciliation Commission to "enable South Africans to come to terms with their past on a morally accepted basis and to advance the cause of reconciliation."[14] Mandela forgave the promoters of discrimination that led to his imprisonment of twenty-six years, and emerged as one of the greatest examples of reconciliation in current times.[15]

On April 20, 1999, Mark Taylor was a student in Columbine High School in Littleton, Colorado. He was shot thirteen times by Eric Harris just outside the high school. He has forgiven shooters Harris and Dylan Klebold and their families for the suffering that he experienced at the hands of these two fellow-students. Taylor has written a book, *I Asked, God Answered: a Columbine Miracle,* that addresses his process of forgiving. Taylor now speaks to gang members and Vietnam veterans about forgiveness.[16]

In the fall of 2007, the tiny Amish community of Nickel Mines, Pennsylvania, was stricken with tragedy. An armed man stormed into a one-room schoolhouse and shot ten little girls before taking his own life. Five of these young girls died within hours, while

13. "Elisabeth Elliot," see http://www.elisabethelliot.org/about.html accessed February 7, 2009.

14. From http://www.doj.gov.za/trc/ accessed July 3, 2009.

15. BBC Online Network, "Nelson Mandela: Prisoner turned President," accessed February 1, 2009, at http://news.bbc.co.uk/1/hi/special_report /1998/10 /98/truth_and_reconcilition/202394.stm.

16. Howard Pankratz, "Columbine Victim Teaches Forgiveness," from *The Denver Post* newspaper, posted 12/06/06, accessed February 2, 2009 at http://www.denverpost.com/ci_4785612.

the others clung to life. Just one day after some of the Amish families had buried their murdered daughters, and the fate of the others remained uncertain, they attended the funeral of the killer. Some of them hugged the widow and the other members of the killer's family. A year later, the Amish community donated money to the killer's widow and her three young children as an act of love and demonstration of their forgiveness toward the killer.[17] Forgiveness is at the very center of the Amish culture. Although they continued to suffer from the loss of their beloved children, they forgave the killer and bestowed great love on his family.

The list of people who have forgiven the perpetrators of atrocities could go on and on. We find it almost impossible to understand how any of these persons, whose hurts were so deep, could forgive those who inflicted such trauma upon them and those they loved. We shy away from the reality that ordinary people can suffer extreme injustices and devastation and still forgive. Yet from a place of hurt, anger, suffering, and despair these people learned how to live transformed lives that embodied forgiveness of others. This is not a utopian ideal, but the Kingdom of God at work in you and me.

---

17. Joseph Shapiro, "Amish Forgive School Shooter, Struggle with Grief," NPR, accessed February 1, 2009 at   http://www.npr.org/templates/story/story.php?storyId=14900930. Also, note book by Donald Kraybill, Steven M. Nolt, and David L. Weaver-Zercher, *Amish Grace: How Forgiveness Transcends Tragedy* (San Francisco, CA: Jossey-Bass, 2007).

Chapter 11

The Recapitulation

Love Is Paramount

When a learned Pharisee asked Jesus, "Teacher, which is the greatest commandment in the Law?" (Matt 22:36), Jesus responded, "Love the Lord your God with all your heart and with all your soul and with all your mind. This is the first and the greatest commandment. And the second is like it: 'Love your neighbor as yourself'" (Matt 22:37-40). Forgiveness is a central component of Christian love. When we love God, we are grateful for the merciful relationship that he maintains with us despite the fact that we repeatedly fall short of the mark. When we love our neighbors as ourselves, we want to be merciful to them amidst, and in spite of their flaws. As we embark on a short review of the processes described in this book, we begin with the one on which all others depend. A heart that is settled on loving God and others is an essential prerequisite to transformation through forgiveness. Hopefully, this recap will draw your attention to areas of your life that deserve affirmation as well as areas in which you are being challenged to live differently from the past.

God's Initiation Is the Foundation of Forgiveness

The biblical record includes many examples of God's acts of initiation with us. Our creation in his image, the deliverance of Israel from slavery in Egypt, the giving of the Ten Commandments, the provision of the sacrificial system and temple worship, coming among us in the person of Jesus and the Holy Spirit, and the establishment of the Church are but a few examples of God reaching out to a fallen world. The Old Testament records that God continually drew near to Israel so that his people might draw near to him. "They will know that I am the Lord their God, who brought them out of Egypt so that I might dwell among them. I am the Lord their God" (Exod 29:45-46). God's initiation with his people stems from his love for them.

God's initiation has two purposes. One is to express his love for us by being with us, even before we can respond. The second is to demonstrate the nature of love so that we might initiate loving relationships with one another. As we experience God's love, we increasingly comprehend his call to love one another in the same way that he loves us. This two-fold purpose is rooted in the two commandments with which we began this chapter.[1]

Christians believe that God's greatest act of initiation was sending his Son Jesus to die for us. Under the old covenant, the ongoing problem of sin made necessary the repetition of rites of cleansing and consecration year after year.[2] Now the blood of Jesus provides a once-for-all time cleansing and consecration to the service of God.[3] The sacrifice of Christ is foundational to a Christian theology of forgiveness and reconciliation because it is "by the blood of Jesus" that we are able to approach God[4] and share in the Son's relationship with the Father.

Our postmodern Western culture no longer includes the remembrance of God's saving and forgiving acts in our collective memory. Instead, we have taken on a vision of self-sufficiency and fierce independence. We see ourselves, not God, as the arbiters of truth and justice. These views reinforce the notion that we are authorized to set the terms of forgiveness. Thus, the Christian is constantly

---

1. See Matt 22:37-40.
2. See Heb 10:1-4.
3. See Heb 9:14, 10:12, 13:12.
4. See Heb 10:19. 7:25.

challenged to choose between this human vision and God's vision—in the marketplace, in politics, in the field of education, and in the arts. Jesus was similarly challenged to make a decisive choice when he was tested in the wilderness.[5] He did not follow cultural trends in making his decision about his relationship with his Father. Neither should we. We must reject every alternative to God's claim on our exclusive devotion and loyalty.

Responding to God's initiative in salvation and revelation and doing so in the way that he requires is the basis of acceptable worship under both the Old Testament and New Testament covenants.[6] In New Testament terms, worship means responding with one's whole life and being to the divine kingship of Jesus.[7] In his letter to the Romans, Paul exhorts believers to hate what is evil, cling to what is good, and be devoted to one another in brotherly love. In Romans 12, he explains that true worship is exhibited in a lifestyle of Christ-like character and service to others in response to God's initiative and Jesus' sacrifice for us. As Christians, our lives and our spoken affirmations need to spring from the reality of our forgiveness through Christ alone. What religious activities strain to achieve has been fulfilled once and for all by Christ's life, death, resurrection, and ascension. Theologian Robert Taft writes, "Christian worship is not how we seek to contact God; it is a celebration of how God has touched us, has united us to himself and is ever present to us and dwelling with us."[8] Just as the Jewish Passover reenacts the saving event of the Passover, Christian worship reenacts the saving events of Christ's life.

---

5. See Matt 4:8-10.
6. David Peterson, *Engaging with God* (Downer's Grove, IL: InterVarsity Press, 1992), 19.
7. Ibid., 144.
8. Robert Taft, "187–Liturgical Worship: Enactment of Salvation History" in *The Complete Library of Christian Worship*, vol. 2, *Twenty Centuries of Christian Worship*, Robert E. Webber, ed. (Peabody, MA: Hendrickson Publishers, Inc., 1994), 269.

Christian spiritual formation is a mere chimera when we rely upon anything other than *God's* revealed plan of forgiveness for humanity and his revealed process of forgiveness and reconciliation with one another.

Forgiveness of Others

Just as God initiated forgiveness with us, we, too, are told to extend forgiveness to everyone we encounter. As God's ambassadors we establish the credibility of God's forgiveness only as we exhibit the realities of forgiveness in our own lives. Our motivation to forgive stems not only from obedience to God's call, but also from knowing that God has freely given to us. We know that we have not earned forgiveness and so we forgive others, granting that they, too, need not earn it.

Forgiveness requires us to cancel our expectation that others must behave a certain way before we will love and forgive them. It means we set aside the option of revenge when we are hurt. Forgiveness is entering into a process, not a one-time declaration. Forgiveness is born from a series of intermediate choices. For instance, when we pray for and bless those who hurt us, we move a long distance toward forgiving them.

Persevering in the process of forgiveness is not easy. Unfortunately, most of us hold in our memories a collection of detailed scripts from the many times we have been hurt by others. In a flash we can recall the cast of characters and feel the intensity of our pain. Yet, if we wait for those who have hurt us to ask to be forgiven, we make ourselves hostages to the very people who have wronged us.[9] When we take the initiative to forgive them, we are the prisoner who is set free from captivity. Initiating forgiveness does not guarantee that the relationships will be restored; rather it provides the opportunity for healing to begin.

---

9. Lewis Smedes, *Forgive and Forget: Healing the Hurt We Don't Deserve* (San Francisco, CA: Harper, 1984), X.

Christians are called to initiate the process of forgiveness, whether we are the one who has been hurt, or the one who is the perpetrator. If we know that someone has something against us, whether real or perceived, we are to initiate attempts to reconcile, confessing and repenting from anything we have done wrong. When we approach those we have hurt or those who have hurt us, we build a bridge that we hope they will choose to cross, bringing restoration to our broken relationship.

The historic Christian perspectives regarding forgiveness may not only seem unfamiliar, but unnatural as well. The principle of unconditional forgiveness is squarely in conflict with the Western contemporary conviction that we need to forgive someone only after they have sought forgiveness from us. From this point of view, we might decide not to forgive at all. Such behavior is utterly destructive.

It takes courage to venture into this unknown territory. To forgive others as Christ has forgiven us, requires that we reject the norms of a large portion of society. This way of life is counter-cultural. You will have chosen to appear peculiar, immature, or dysfunctional to others. In order to step into the lifestyle of healed relationships, we each must step outside the popular cultural understanding of forgiveness and into this counter-cultural view. This step will be a tough move, because many of our peers, both secular and Christian, will disagree. We can expect little support from others. Yet, character which is above reproach, quick to forgive, and based in loving servanthood is to be the distinction of our entire lives as Christians, with all people, in all contexts, whether we are loved, hated, revered, or despised.

Forgive without Judgment

The ancient texts presented in previous chapters provide us with examples of early Christians gently confronting sinful behavior in one another. Though Jesus encouraged such conversations, this does not imply his approval for expressions of condemnation or shame. Condemnation impedes reconciliation at least as much as a lack of repentance or refusal of forgiveness. Condemning attitudes are prideful and self-exalting, and should be resisted. When he addressed the woman who had been caught committing adultery "Jesus straightened up and asked her, 'Woman, where are they? Has no one condemned you?' 'No one, sir,' she said. 'Then neither do I condemn you,' Jesus declared. 'Go now and leave your life of sin'" (John 8:10-11). Instead of condemnation, Jesus offered mercy to her. In the same way, we are never to shame others because of their sinfulness.[10]

Announcing to someone, who has offended us, that we forgive them can be a subtle form of condemnation. An unsolicited "I forgive you" is not usually received as a word of love and reconciliation. Instead, this proclamation can be very hurtful, and often is a transparent mask for our condemnation of the other persons. If so, articulating our 'forgiveness' is self-serving, if not self-righteous. Such an announcement could easily enflame one who does not see his or her own shortcomings, thus delaying the reconciliation that would honor God. There is no wisdom in *telling* anyone that we have forgiven them unless they have asked us to do so. Addressing this view, James Torrance writes, "Sensing the element of judgment, of condemnation in the word, he might well reject the forgiveness, because he refuses to submit to the verdict of guilty implied in it."[11] The better path is to resist the temptation to unburden ourselves at another's expense. Instead, we can implement a condemnation-free loving attitude toward the one who has caused us pain, in hope that he or she might become motivated to reconsider past actions and seek reconciliation. Implicit in a desire for reconciliation is the

---

10. Phil Maxwell, "Repentance, Forgiveness, Reconciliation & Condemnation: There's a difference," accessed 20 October 2005, found at http://www.planetkc.com/stm/condemn.htm.
11. James B. Torrance, *Worship, Community, & Triune God of Grace* (Downer's Grove, IL: InterVarsity Press, 1996), 55.

acceptance of our love and forgiveness, along with his or her unspoken submission to the verdict of guilty. Should this happen, both persons will experience a major transformation. If reconciliation does not come, at least we will not be the obstacle prolonging the fractured relationship.

Confession

Confession is agreeing with God's point of view. It is much broader than simply admitting what we have done wrong, and involves confessing Jesus as well as confessing to Jesus. Confession is the means of our participation in Jesus' fellowship with the Father and the crux of our spirituality. This spirituality begins with trust in Jesus, rather than in all the good things we do. When we confess to Jesus, we not only agree with God's point of view about our actions, we also take responsibility for our actions. When we confess to the one we have hurt, we agree with their point of view, insofar as it is true. We cannot expect God to help us modify our behavior unless we first acknowledge our misbehavior. This involves seeking reconciliation with those who feel hurt by us, even if we are not certain we have done anything wrong. When we show mercy to those who seek our forgiveness, we become agents of blessing and open the door to a restored relationship. Christians need to restore the practice of confession, both for the sake of those of us who have been hurt and for the sake of those of us who have hurt others.

Repentance

As we confess God, we are moved by God toward repentance. In the stories of the football player and the driver on the Interstate highway, we recall that both repented. They turned around. A Christian about-face is always toward God and away from destructive urges.

Christian repentance is never simply a reversal of our outward misbehavior, but starts with a fundamental change of heart.

This change of heart leads to new ways of responding to others and a lifestyle of repenting, forgiving, and reconciling. A lifestyle of repentance can have a far reaching impact on those in our circles of influence and help bring restoration to God's fallen creation. A lifestyle of repentance is the key to the spiritual transformation of communities as well as individuals. Christian communities formed around lifestyle repentance experience true spiritual worship of God and make disciples who can truly live a forgiving and reconciling life.

Concluding Thoughts

When we examine the many passages of Scripture, history, and stories presented throughout this book, we sense the urgency to repair broken relationships. We feel encouraged to give our immediate attention to issues of forgiveness, without procrastination.

Both persons involved in a conflicted relationship must resist the temptation to be passive. We are to seek reconciliation with those who accuse us of wrongdoing and forgive those who have sinned against us, just as God forgives us.[12] It makes absolutely no difference whether we are the innocent victim, the perpetrator, or the perceived perpetrator who is actually innocent. We are, insofar as possible, to live at peace with one another.[13] Seeking peace with one another takes precedence over acts of worship! Indeed, an ongoing commitment to reconciliation with others is a core element of true worship. Forgiveness is an essential part of God's plan for the restoration of his creation. There are no seasons of exemption for forgiving others.

The urgency to forgive is intensified when we grasp the reality that our own reconciliation with God is completely interconnected with forgiving others. As we come to understand the way God loves and forgives us, we see how we are to love and forgive others in the same fashion. As we extend and receive graceful forgiveness and

---

12. Matt 5:25.
13. Rom 12:17-19.

experience reconciliation with another person, we come to better comprehend and appreciate the loving God who created us. These are not two distinctly separate processes. If we are truly living out the greatest commandment of loving God with our whole self, then we will live out the second greatest commandment, to love one another as ourselves.

Our forgiveness of others is never to be conditional. Unconditional forgiveness draws us to confession, repentance, and reconciliation. But even if those who have hurt us never recognize their sins, there will never come a time when it is appropriate to retaliate or to condemn and shame them. When we live in this counter-cultural way, we will be misunderstood and unappreciated by our society. Nevertheless, we will be transformed, and that is its own reward.

While we may agree that forgiveness is urgent, important and unconditional, it is only when we move beyond the cognitive and yield our hearts to the truth that we can finally be transformed. Forgiveness is not an analytical problem, but a spiritual process. Transformation comes from God's work in us, not from our own formulaic attempts at behavior modification. Transformed behavior comes from a transformed heart.

So each one of us is responsible to move beyond the cognitive and initiate forgiveness. Consider those from whom you are estranged or with whom you are experiencing conflict. Are there people who trigger in you an urge to repay their deeds with some form of retaliation? Those are the relationships in which to begin striving toward forgiveness and reconciliation. We remember that "while we were still sinners, Christ died for us" (Rom 5:8).

Love someone today as Christ loved you. Become sensitive to those moments when love turns to hate, admiration to envy, and intervention becomes vengeful retaliation. Such awareness is from the Holy Spirit and is an opportunity to enter the transformational process of forgiveness, confession, and repentance.

Key Elements in Transformational Forgiveness

• Respond to God
• Love others
• Extend forgiveness
• Shift to God's point of view
• Confess
• Commit to the community
• Repent
• Be reconciled

The vision of our lives, our mantra, must become *Soli Deo Gloria*—for the glory of God alone. For ancient Christians, living in reconciliation with God and with their brothers and sisters within the church was the passion of their entire lives. A return to these fundamentals will bless God and exhibit his reality and glory to the world. The challenge before us is to passionately extend to others the same forgiving grace God extends to us. Walking through our fears and out of our comfort zones, we are to move into a radical experience of Christ that generates spiritual authenticity no matter the circumstances.

> *Now may the God of peace, who through*
> *the blood of the eternal covenant brought*
> *back from the dead our Lord Jesus, that*
> *great Shepherd of the sheep, equip you*
> *with everything good for doing his will,*
> *and may he work in us what is pleasing*
> *to him, through Jesus Christ, to whom be*
> *the glory for ever and ever. Amen.*
> —Hebrews 13: 20-21

Appendix

Forgiveness: Unleashing a Transformational Process Study Guide[1]

I have developed this study guide to encourage and facilitate personal application of what I have presented in this book. It is organized in a series of eight sessions to be used in individual or group study. Each session tracks with certain sections of the book. The questions are not the simple open-book-look-up-the-answers type. Intended to be thought-provoking, the questions will help you incorporate and expand upon the teaching in this book. For group discussion, select only a few questions from those provided to ensure that your group will have time for in-depth discussion. Everyone should have a copy of the discussion questions.

This study guide will require you to examine your heart, mind, will, and emotions. Strive to be honest about what the Scriptures presented actually say and let them confront you with challenging truths. I hope that you will wrestle with the questions and that your thinking crystallizes answers through this process. Pace your discussion so you will not be rushed.

1. This Study Guide is copyrighted by Adoration Publishing Company, Denver, Colorado, USA in 2010. Adoration Publishing grants the purchasers of this book permission to reproduce this Study Guide for their own use and for all those who would be studying this book with them. All other rights are reserved worldwide.

Each session includes two sets of questions. The first set is for general group discussion. Because not everything personal can or should be shared in a group setting, I have provided a second set of more intimate questions for individual consideration. That way you may disclose your responses to others only if you desire to do so.

I suggest that each group participant read the appropriate sections of the book and answer the questions prior to each of the sessions. When each person allows sufficient time for reading and answering the questions prior to your meeting, the entire group will benefit. It might be helpful for each person to keep a notebook of thoughts about the readings and the responses to the study questions, which he or she can periodically review. This enables deeper engagement and provides a record of how their perspectives change through the study.

Your group facilitator might wish summarize the contents of the reading before moving to the discussion questions. I suggest that you allow some time for each person to share about their Christian formation process. As you participate in the discussion, strive to implement the forgiving lifestyle with one another, which Jesus describes. Engage one another's thoughts and experiences of forgiveness and spiritual formation.

Week 1—Innovative Forgiveness

For this session, please read the Introduction and chapter 1, pages 1-23.

Group Discussion

1. In what ways is the thought about seeing how you fit into God's story (rather than fitting God into your story) new to you? Do you think this is an important perspective to have? Why or why not?

2. How might seeing your story through God's eyes or the eyes of another person help you better address a conflicted relationship?

3. Have you ever been the recipient of unconditional forgiveness from someone you harmed? If so, consider sharing with the group the impact this had upon you. How did the person's forgiveness help you to come to grips with your actions?

4. What conditions do you wish you could put upon other people in order to forgive them?

5. Have you ever encountered someone like Rick (pages 19-20)? What were the most challenging aspects of the relationship for you? What do you now wish you could have done differently?

6. What do you believe caused Pastor Jim's transformation (pages 20-21)? Why might this transformation have been difficult for him to experience?

7. What was the origin and process of the author's personal transformation (pages 7-11)?

8. What type of transformation through forgiveness would you like to experience?

9. Describe how your Christian community understands the process of receiving forgiveness from God. How

does that process compare to what is presented in this chapter?

10. What is your understanding of the process of forgiving someone who has hurt you?

Private Deliberation

1. What examples of 'acceptable' retaliation have you engaged in toward people who have caused you pain?

2. List a few areas where you would like to experience transformation and learn something new about forgiveness.

3. Recall a previous experience when someone you loved caused you great personal pain by his or her actions.
   a. What were your initial reactions?
   b. Did your relationship recover from the trauma? Why or why not?
   c. Pray to God that you might develop or increase your love toward that person.
   d. When you are ready to do so, what actions of love might you initiate toward them?

Week 2—The Meaning of Forgiveness

For this session, please read chapter 2, pages 25-42.

Group Discussion

1. Catharine Dooley (page 25-26) makes a bold statement, "Forgiveness is a difficult process because it is unconditional." What feelings and attitudes would you need to change to be able to imagine yourself always giving forgiveness to those who hurt you?

2. Edith Stauffer (page 27) states that forgiveness means canceling the mental and emotional demands that we have decided must be honored before we will give our love. What are some of the expectations a person would have to eliminate to become free to extend love to someone who hurts them?

3. Summarize the distinction C. S. Lewis (page 28-30) makes between presenting excuses and seeking forgiveness. Be prepared to restate his perspective in a few sentences. How might this perspective diminish our reluctance to forgive others?

4. Recall the trauma caused to Joseph (pages 30-32 and Gen 37-50) by his brothers. What was the agenda of the brothers? When his brothers came to Egypt for food, how did Joseph's frame of reference form his responses?

5. Read John 14:6 and the discussion on page 36-38. What is your initial response to this? Explain in several sentences what you think Jesus is communicating. Do you believe that Jesus is the only way to God? Why or why not?

6. Review Ephesians 2:4-9 and Romans 5:8 (page 38-39). What is the basis on which we receive God's offer of forgiveness? When do you find it especially difficult to depend on this basis for forgiveness?

Private Deliberation

1. Identify a hurtful series of events inflicted on you by someone you loved (as happened to Joseph).
   a. What did they do to you?
   b. What was your perspective as the events unfolded?
   c. How did you relate afterward to the events and those who caused them?
   d. Use your imagination to write a paragraph about the situation from God's point of view.
   e. What might God have you do differently?

Week 3—The Role and Characteristics of Forgiveness

For this session, please read chapters 3-4, pages 43-66.

Group Discussion

1. Review the third-century process for being accepted for baptism. (See pages 43-45.) How does this contrast with the practice today in your church? What are the potential benefits and dangers of the ancient way compared to your church's way?

2. When we pray the Lord's prayer (page 48-49), we ask for forgiveness and in the same breath, we declare that we have forgiven all who have hurt us. How does this reality affect your anticipation of forgiveness by God?

3. Consider the example of forgiveness that is given in Ephesians 4:32 (pages 51-52). What do you understand this verse to mean?

4. Review the parable of the unmerciful servant (pages 55-57 and Matthew 18:21-35). Why do you suppose the one who had been forgiven so much would not extend forgiveness to one who owed him so little? What point do you think Jesus was making in this parable?

5. What circumstances would move you to intervene with a Christian living in a way unbecoming to a believer? How would you know when to mind your own business? What actions on your part would be appropriate for your intervention? Inappropriate?

6. In John 17 (pages 65-66) Jesus prays that all who believe in him would love one another and be unified. What is the difference between unity and uniformity? What does Jesus say are the consequences of Christian unity? Describe a time when you encountered this consequence of unity. How could a person in your situation take initiative to help increase Christian unity?

Personal Deliberation

1. Name any people you know who might have personal issues with you. How have you experienced distance in these relationships?

2. What does Scripture ask you to do, now that you have identified these restricted relationships? How can you take one step toward accomplishing this?

3. Read the parable of the unmerciful servant again (Matt 18:21-35, discussed on pages 55-57). What would you have to give up to live in a way that would conform to Jesus' teaching?

Week 4—Forgiveness as Worship and the Myths of Forgiveness

For this session, please read chapters 5-6, pages 67-79.

Group Discussion

1. List the different ways forgiveness is an act of worship (chapter 5). Which ones are new ideas for you? Do you have doubts or questions about anything on your list? Explain. If you could forgive someone you have yet to forgive, how do you imagine that could change your worship of God?

2. Both worship and forgiveness begin within the heart and then move to action. How have you experienced this? How would you encourage someone to begin, if he or she was struggling to forgive?

3. Of the thirteen fictional myths about forgiveness that I have presented in the book (pages 71-79), which ones brought you some relief and encouragement? In what way? Of the myths presented, are there any you believe are true? Why?

4. How does Myth #2 (page 72) reinforce what C. S. Lewis wrote about forgiveness (pages 28-29)?

5. If you would add any other fictional myths to the list, what would they be?

Personal Deliberation

1. Have any of these thirteen myths immobilized your ability to receive forgiveness from someone? Which one(s)? With whom? How might you be liberated from this stress?

2. Have any of these thirteen myths immobilized your ability to forgive someone? Which one(s)? With whom? Brainstorm ideas that would help you become liberated

enough to make the first step toward forgiveness. Choose one idea to implement.

3. How can you change your worship practices to help you in your struggle with giving or receiving forgiveness?

Week 5—Confession

For this session, please read chapter 7, pages 81-97.

Group Discussion

1. The word 'confession', as used in the Scriptures, has two different meanings (see pages 82-86). What are they? How do they differ from one another? How do they intersect with one another?

2. Examine the ancient confessions presented on pages 86-92. What did you notice that was new or surprising?

3. The Nicene Creed was composed to specifically address a number of 'innovative' theologies that were creeping into Christian churches. Discuss ways this creed challenges the popular thinking within your Christian group. (Note, I am talking about how people really think, believe, and behave, not what the 'party line' is within your church.)

4. Most people understand lament to mean feeling sorry for yourself. Review Psalm 51 and discuss the possible end results of biblical lament.

5. What are ineffective ways to ask for forgiveness? What specific Scriptures can you think of that describe or imply effective ways of asking for forgiveness?

6. When you come to realize that someone has something against you but has not come to you to seek reconciliation, what is your role in the process? If they are unwilling to discuss it with you, what will you do?

Personal Deliberation

1. As you pray through the General Confession (pages 90-91), what does the Lord bring to mind for you to confess? Is there anything different from past moments of private prayer? Describe it.

2. Select an area of personal pain or unresolved sin and go through the biblical process of lament explained in pages 92-95. Afterwards, reflect on what God did in your heart. Consider sharing your experience with a trusted friend.

3. Is there anyone who has something against you? What do you think you need to do?

Week 6—Repentance

For this session, please read chapter 8, pages 99-121.

Group Discussion

1. Do you agree that outer change inevitably follows inner change? Why or why not?

2. Think of a time when you primarily focused on changing your behavior and hoped that your heart would follow. Was that process effective or not? Describe how and why.

3. What constructive steps can a person take to begin changing his or her heart and mind? How does this differ from striving to change one's behavior through discipline and accountability alone?

4. Review William Temple's explanation of John 15 (page 117). How does he describe the process of 'bearing fruit'? What might this new fruit look like in our lives?

5. In your experience, what are some significant consequences of repentance? Look again at Matthew 7:1-6 and pages 106-107. How does your idea square with these ideas?

6. Review Isaiah 1:14-20 (pages 110-111). The prophet Isaiah described what spiritual-looking activity from which God's people needed to repent?

7. Think of religious-like activity in which you have been engaged that does not accomplish Christian formation in you. What would it look like for you to repent from this counterfeit spirituality?

Personal Deliberation

1. Repentance is a change from one intention to a distinctively different intention.
    a. Name one or two areas in the past, where you have repented.
    b. If you had not 'turned about', what would have happened?
2. Summarize Calvin's reframing of repentance (pages 114-115). In order for you to live the way of repentance, what do you need to change?
3. Think of one area of your life where you believe God would have you live differently (repent). What would you like to change? How could you begin the process of repentance within your heart?

Week 7—Reconciliation

For this session, please read chapter 9, pages 123-137.

Group Discussion

1. Review the parable of the Prodigal Son (Luke 15, pages 126-129).
   a. Describe the virtues that you see in the younger son. What kept him from returning home earlier? What needed to happen for him to return to his father?
   b. Describe the virtues that you see in the loving father. What evidence is there that he was loving and forgiving?
   c. Describe the perspectives of the older brother. What changes would he need to make to be reconciled to his father?
2. What is necessary for true reconciliation?
3. Review the image of the grapes and the grain found on pages 130-132. How does this relate to the concept of Christian community?
4. What works against becoming a connected part of a Christian community? Why is it easier to remain an onlooker from a guarded distance? How could your group eliminate one barrier that keeps people away?

Private Deliberation

1. What qualities of love and forgiveness draw others to you? In whom do you see the qualities of love and forgiveness? How might you gain insight from this person to maximize these qualities in your own life?
2. In what areas of your life have you taken on the role of the prodigal son?
3. In what ways have you been the older brother?
4. Where have you acted as the loving father?

5. Who could benefit if you were to behave as the loving father toward them?

6. Think of a person who would be encouraged if you initiated reconciliation with them. What is keeping you from taking that initiative now?

7. Identify a 'neighbor' that you do not know. What steps could you take to meet and serve this person, remembering your role as an 'ambassador of love'?

Week 8—Reclaiming Forgiveness

For this session, please read chapters 10-11, pages 139-162.

Group Discussion

1. What formulas have you encountered that people use to gain forgiveness? What portions of those formulas are partially correct? What important elements do you believe are missing from these formulas?
2. What fears keep people from initiating forgiveness? What steps could a person take to move through these fears?
3. From the discussion of Apollo 11 (pages 142-145) what new thoughts do you have about the process of forgiving others?
4. Review Matthew 22:36, page 153.
    a. What passions motivated God to offer his Son in order that we might experience forgiveness?
    b. What passion would motivate you to forgive someone?
5. Do you think forgiveness, confession, repentance, and reconciliation are unavoidably connected? Can one be separated from another? Why or why not?
6. As you review your notes about forgiveness, what have you learned that surprised you?

Private Deliberation

1. In what broken relationships do you see no hope of reconciliation, apart from an intervention by God? What do you believe is blocking reconciliation? Identify any action you can take, as an act of worship, which would communicate your willingness to be reconciled with that person?
2. What circumstances are in your life which you can now see from God's point of view (theocentric) which in the

past you have primarily viewed from your own point of view (anthropocentric)? What are the circumstances you would like to see from God's point of view, instead of your own?

3. As you remember that true knowing is experienced in a person's heart and life, what dimensions of forgiveness do you desire to know in a deeper way?

Selected Bibliography

Allen, Clifton J., ed. *The Broadman Bible Commentary,* vol. 8-9. Nashville, TN: Broadman Press, 1969.

Allison, C. Fitzsimons. *The Cruelty of Heresy: An Affirmation of Christian Orthodoxy.* Harrisburg, PA: Morehouse Publishing, 1994.

Anderson, Leith. *A Church for the Twenty-First Century.* Minneapolis, MN: Bethany House, 1992.

Aulen, Gustaf. *Christus Victor.* Eugene, OR: Wipf & Stock Publishers, 2003 (also 1931).

Bettenson, Henry and Chris Maunder, ed. *Documents of the Christian Church.* Oxford: Oxford Press, 1943.

Barna, George. *The Frog in the Kettle: What Christians Need to Know About Life in the Year 2000.* Ventura, CA: Regal Books, 1990.

Beazley, Hamilton. *No Regrets: A Ten-Step Program for Living in the Present and Leaving the Past Behind.* Hoboken, NJ: John Wiley & Sons, Inc., 2004.

The Book of Common Prayer. New York, NY: Church Hymnal Corporation, 1979.

Borchert, Gerald L. *Worship in the New Testament.* St. Louis, MO: Chalice Press, 2008.

_____. *Assurance and Warning*. Singapore: Word N Works, 2006.

Brand, Chad, Charles Draper, Archie England, gen. ed. *Holman Illustrated Bible Dictionary*. Nashville, TN: Holman Bible Publishers, 2003.

Brown, Colin, ed. *The New International Dictionary of New Testament Theology*, vol.1 and 2. Grand Rapids, MI: Zondervan, 1986.

Brown, Peter. *The Making of Late Antiquity*. Cambridge, MA: Harvard University Press, 1978.

The Calvin Institute of Christian Worship. *The Worship Sourcebook*. Grand Rapids, MI: The Calvin Institute for Worship, 2004. (Co-published also with Grand Rapids, MI: Faith Alive Christian Resources, 2004 and Grand Rapids, MI: Baker Books, 2004).

Dix, Gregory. *The Apostolic Tradition of St. Hippolytus*. London: Society for Promoting Christian Knowledge, 1937.

_____. *The Shape of the Liturgy*. London: Continuum, 1945, 2003.

Dooley, Catherine. "Theology of Forgiveness" in *The New Dictionary of Sacramental Worship*. Collegeville, MN: The Liturgical Press, 1990.

Essig, Montgomery F. *The Comprehensive Analysis of the Bible*. Nashville, TN: The Southwestern Company, 1951.

Fink, Peter E., ed. *The New Dictionary of Sacramental Worship*. Collegeville, MN: The Liturgical Press, 1990.

Hatchett, Marion J. *Commentary on the American Prayer Book.* New York, NY: HarperCollins Publishers, 1995.

The Holy Bible, Today's New International Version. Grand Rapids, MI: Zondervan, 2006.

Kendall, R.T. *Total Forgiveness.* Lake Mary, FL: Charisma House, 2007.

Kleist, James A., S.J., Ph.D., trans. *"The Didache"* from *Ancient Christian Writers,* vol. 6. New York, NY: The Newman Press, 1948.

Kraybill, Donald, Steven M. Nolt, and David L. Weaver-Zercher. *Amish Grace: How Forgiveness Transcends Tragedy.* San Francisco, CA: Jossey-Bass, 2007.

Lake, Kirsopp, Translator. *The Didache: The Teaching of the Twelve Apostles.* Martinez, CA: St. Columbia Press, 1912.

LaVerdiere, Eugene, S.S.S. *Luke.* Wilmington, DE: Michael Glazier, Inc., 1980.

Lewis, C. S. "Forgiveness," from *The Weight of Glory and Other Addresses.* New York, NY: HarperCollins Publishers, Inc., 2000.

Lyotard, Jean-Francois. *The Postmodern Condition: A Report on Knowledge* (Theory and History of Literature). Minneapolis, MN: University of Minnesota Press, 1984.

Maxwell, Phil. *Repentance, Forgiveness, Reconciliation, & Condemnation: There's a difference.* http://www.planetkc.com/stm/condemn.htm, 1998.

Meninger, William A. *The Process of Forgiveness.* New York, NY: Continuum International Publishing Group, 1996.

Nash, Robert N., *An 8-Track Church in a CD World: The Modern Church in the Postmodern World.* Macon, GA: Smyth & Helwys Publishing, Inc., 1997.

Nicoll, W. Robertson. *The Expositor's Greek Testament,* vol. 1. New York, NY: George H. Doran Company, 1917.

Niederwimmer, Kurt. *The Didache.* Minneapolis, MN: Fortress Press, 1998.

Peterson, David. *Engaging with God.* Downers Grove, IL: InterVarsity Press, 1992.

Schwandt, John, ed. *The English-Greek Reverse Interlinear New Testament.* Wheaton, IL: Crossway Books, 2006.

Smedes, Lewis S. *The Art of Forgiving: When You Need to Forgive and Don't Know How.* New York, NY: Ballantine Books, 1996.

Smedes, Lewis S. *Forgive and Forget: Healing the Hurt We Don't Deserve.* New York, NY: HarperCollins Publishers, 1984.

Smith, Chuck, Jr. *The End of the World as We Know It.* Colorado Springs, CO: WaterBook Press, 2001.

Stauffer, Edith R., Ph.D. *Unconditional Love and Forgiveness.* Diamond Springs, CA: Triangle Publishers, 1987.

Sweet, Leonard. *Post-Modern Pilgrims: First Century Passion for the 21st Century World.* Nashville, TN: Broadman & Holman Publishers, 2000.

Temple, William. *Readings in St. John's Gospel* (First and Second Series). London: MacMillan and Co., Limited, 1953.

ten Boom, Corrie. *Tramp for the Lord.* Old Tappan, NJ: Fleming H. Revel Company, 1974.

Tenney, Merrill C. *The Zondervan Pictorial Dictionary.* Grand Rapids, MI: Zondervan Publishing House, 1967.

Torrance, James B. Worship, *Community & the Triune God of Grace.* Downers Grove, IL: InterVarsity Press, 1996.

Veith, Gene Edward, Jr. *Postmodern Times: A Christian Guide to Contemporary Thought and Culture.* Wheaton, IL: Crossway Books, 1994.

Vine, W. E. *Vine's Expository Dictionary of Old and New Testament Words.* Old Tappan, NJ: Fleming H. Revell Company, 1981.

Webber, Robert E. *Ancient-Future Faith: Rethinking Evangelicalism for a Postmodern World.* Grand Rapids, MI: Baker Books, 1999.

_____. *Ancient-Future Worship: Proclaiming and Enacting God's Narrative.* Grand Rapids, MI: Baker Books, 2008.

_____, Editor. *The Complete Library of Christian Worship,* vol. 1, *Twenty Centuries of Christian Worship.* Peabody, MA: Hendrickson Publishers, Inc., 1993.

_____. *The Complete Library of Christian Worship,* vol. 2, *Twenty Centuries of Christian Worship.* Peabody, MA: Hendrickson Publishers, Inc., 1994.

_____. *The Divine Embrace.* Grand Rapids, MI: Baker Books, 2006.

White, James F. *A Brief History of Christian Worship.* Nashville, TN: Abingdon Press, 1993.

_____. *Protestant Worship: Traditions in Transition.* Louisville, KY: Westminster/John Knox Press, 1989.

_____. *Introduction to Christian Worship.* Nashville, TN: Abingdon Press, 2000.

Wilford, John Noble. 1969. "The Mission Apollo 11: On the Moon." *Look Magazine.* New York, NY: Cowles Communications Inc., 1969.

Index of Subjects

Index of Persons

Index of Scriptures

LaVergne, TN USA
30 March 2010
177561LV00002B/3/P